A Guide to Historic
BOZEMAN

*The City of Bozeman and the Montana Preservation Alliance
provided funding for this project.*

MONTANA MAINSTREETS
VOLUME 7

A Guide to Historic
BOZEMAN

BY JIM JENKS

Preface by Mark F. Baumler,
State Historic Preservation Officer of Montana

Foreword by Chere Jiusto,
Executive Director, Montana Preservation Alliance

Montana Historical Society Press
Helena, Montana

COVER IMAGE Main Street, Bozeman, c. 1965
Photography courtesy Pioneer Museum, Bozeman
BOOK AND COVER DESIGN DD Dowden, Helena
MAPS Tony Moore, Helena
TYPESET IN Minion
PRINTED IN CANADA BY CREASEY PRINTING

The photographs in this book are from the following sources and are credited using
the following abbreviations: Historic Preservation Office, City of Bozeman (COB);
Gallatin Historical Society and Pioneer Museum (Pioneer Museum); Jim Jenks
(Author); Montana Historical Society (MHS); Museum of the Rockies (MOR).
Line art was drawn by Ken Sievert, Great Falls.

Distributed by Globe Pequot Press, 246 Goose Lane, Guilford, Connecticut 06437
(800) 243-0495

ISBN-13: 978-0-9721522-3-5

ISBN-10: 0-9721522-3-7

07 08 09 10 11 12 13 14 15 16   10 9 8 7 6 5 4 3 2 1

LIBRARY OF CONGRESS CATALOGING-IN-PUBLICATION DATA
Jenks, Jim.
   A guide to historic Bozeman / by Jim Jenks ; with a preface by Mark F. Baumler.
   p. cm.—(Montana mainstreets ; v. 7)
   Includes bibliographical references and index.
   ISBN-13: 978-0-9721522-3-5
   ISBN-10: 0-9721522-3-7
   1. Historic districts—Montana—Bozeman—Guidebooks. 2. Historic sites—Mon-
tana—Bozeman—Guidebooks. 3. Historic buildings—Montana—Bozeman—Guidebooks.
4. Architecture—Montana—Bozeman—Guidebooks. 5. Bozeman (Mont.)—Tours. 6.
Bozeman (Mont.)—Buildings, structures, etc.—Guidebooks. 7. Bozeman (Mont.)—
History. I. Title.
F739.B69J46 2007   200701351
978.6'662—dc22

For my father and in the memory of my mother

CONTENTS

PREFACE

Montana Mainstreets INVITES YOU to take a new look at some of Montana's oldest living towns using historic buildings—businesses, institutions, and homes—to illustrate the story. The information derives from the State Historic Preservation Office's efforts to work with people all across the state to inventory historic places and identify those eligible for listing in the National Register of Historic Places. This work began in the 1970s and continues today.

Some readers may be surprised to learn that historic buildings, perhaps located in their own town, are or could be listed in the National Register. Isn't such designation reserved for architectural masterpieces, the birthplaces of American heroes, the oldest, the biggest, and the best in the nation? While such places often do qualify for recognition, they alone do not comprise the National Register of Historic Places. Beyond great national landmarks, the Register also includes properties of importance to local communities—buildings associated with local and state events and people, homes representative of architectural styles and period craftsmanship, and even archaeological sites that offer important glimpses into places and people no longer visible. The goal of community historic surveys is less about identifying the "top ten" and more about recognizing how buildings, streets, and neighborhoods combine to reflect a town's history and the sense of place of its residents.

In the volumes of the *Montana Mainstreets* series, you will read about communities where history is not only past but also very much present. These are not ghost towns frozen in time; nor is the historic built environment obsolete or abandoned. In these communities, the historic homes and commercial quarters still contribute—economically, socially, politically, and aesthetically—to their town's livelihood and purpose. They are testimonies that historic preservation works and makes sense.

In these slim volumes, not every historic or architecturally significant structure is illustrated, nor can every story be told. Therefore, in addition to providing information on specific properties, these guides are designed to educate readers about local historical trends, styles, and developments and thus to help them better understand other buildings in the featured communities and across the state. The real value is where these books can take you from here.

Among my archaeologist friends there is a saying: Forward into the past! I trust you will heed this invitation in your journey down Montana's historical main streets.

Mark F. Baumler
State Historic Preservation Officer of Montana

FOREWORD

BORN UPSTREAM FROM THE HEADWATERS of the Missouri River, Bozeman is a town shaped by people and the historic currents of exploration, the fur trade, early immigration, agriculture, railroads, and higher learning. These currents carried the community as it grew from a small settlement in the midst of the expansive Gallatin Valley into a prosperous western city with inviting neighborhoods and a vibrant downtown.

Like the three rivers that braid together at the headwaters, Bozeman's homes and buildings reflect a past that is made greater by the joining together of all of their stories. Each building reflects a time when people not so different from us lived and worked, built and hoped and dreamed.

A Guide to Historic Bozeman is seventh in a series that records the stories of individual communities and invites us to explore history in our own backyards. In this book, my colleague Jim Jenks has drawn together the many strands of Bozeman's past and fit them against the backdrop of national events, providing us a narrative for better understanding Montana's history and that of the people who lived here before us.

The Montana Preservation Alliance is pleased to join the City of Bozeman and the Montana Historical Society in this effort to highlight Bozeman's history and to build appreciation for preserving the city's historic places.

Chere Jiusto
Executive Director, Montana Preservation Alliance

ACKNOWLEDGMENTS

LITTLE OF BOZEMAN'S HISTORY could be told without the resources of local museums and libraries. The following repositories and institutions hold extensive collections and are staffed by dedicated professionals and volunteers. These museums and libraries should be lauded for the services they offer and as places where acknowledging our past is everyday business. Most of the sources used in preparing this guidebook are from the following repositories, and I offer thanks to each:

- Gallatin Historical Society and Pioneer Museum
- Merrill G. Burlingame Special Collections, Montana State University
- Montana Historical Society, particularly the State Historic Preservation Office
- Montana Room, Bozeman Public Library
- Museum of the Rockies

The photographic collections of the Gallatin Historical Society and Pioneer Museum, the Montana Historical Society, and Montana State University's Museum of the Rockies were an invaluable resource. My thanks go to the staff who assisted in reviewing the collections.

This guidebook would not have been possible without the research completed by other historians, including Phyllis Smith, Merrill G. Burlingame, and especially B. Derek Strahn. Thanks also to Chere Jiusto and Christine Brown of the Montana Preservation Alliance and Molly Holz and Martha Kohl of the Montana Historical Society for their invaluable assistance and editorial support. The City of Bozeman Office of Planning and Community Development deserves special recognition for providing funding for this book.

HOW TO USE THIS GUIDE

*With a basis of agriculture . . . and water power, the support
of the city must be permanent. When to these are added
superior healthfulness and charming surroundings, with the
further fact that the character of the community is already
established as one of the most moral and intelligent, the most
promising in the state for an educational center, it requires
no spirit of prophecy to forecast a bright future for the city
of Bozeman.*

— J. D. RADFORD AND COMPANY'S *GALLATIN VALLEY
GAZETTEER AND BOZEMAN CITY DIRECTORY, 1892–1895*

A STROLL DOWN BOZEMAN'S MAIN STREET tells much about
how the landscape has changed since John Bozeman visited
the Gallatin Valley in 1864. In just a few decades, the open
range and pristine creeks gave way to plowed fields, irrigation
ditches, and a bustling Main Street as Bozeman became an
agricultural center. Through the years, the college and a burgeoning tourist industry shaped the town in yet other ways.
Bozeman has seen, and been home to, many pasts.

The story of Bozeman's transformation incorporates the
stories of thousands of individuals. We think of their history
as preserved in family documents, photographs, and shared
memories, but it is also preserved in the buildings we walk
past every day. These buildings line the streets of Bozeman's
downtown and older neighborhoods. They are historic touch-

stones, and their connection to the people and events who shaped the city is the subject of this book.

No book this size can be comprehensive—and this guide is not intended to be. Nor is it intended as a site-by-site walking tour. Instead, the book introduces readers to Bozeman's unique history and the way that history is reflected on the landscape. The guide is divided into two sections. The first part of the book provides a brief overview of the significant individuals and social, political, and economic influences that spurred Bozeman's growth—starting in prehistory, proceeding through the late nineteenth and twentieth centuries, and ultimately arriving in the modern day.

The second part of the book takes a closer look at Bozeman's historic architecture, with a special focus on Bozeman's historic districts. Nationally, thousands of historic districts are listed in the National Register of Historic Places, our nation's list of historically significant heritage sites. In Bozeman, over eight hundred National Register listings comprise the city's nine historic districts, one of the highest percentages of historic places located within a single community in the United States. This section fittingly concludes with a look at the growth of historic preservation both nationwide and in Bozeman. Information about Bozeman's most common architectural styles, a time line, and a bibliography round out the book.

To aid the reader, site numbers inserted in boldface in the text (**site 1**) are keyed to maps located throughout the book. The map on page 46 shows the arrangement of Bozeman's National Register districts. Twelve detail maps scattered throughout the book show the location of individual sites.

After reading this book and visiting a few of Bozeman's historic sites, you will be able to discern some of the larger historical trends that shaped the city and recognize the various types of architecture that highlight so much local history. These trends apply to buildings that are mentioned in this guide—and to buildings that are not. Remember, then, as you discover Bozeman, that this book is a mere starting point to exploring the city's lively history.

BOZEMAN AND
SOUTHWESTERN MONTANA

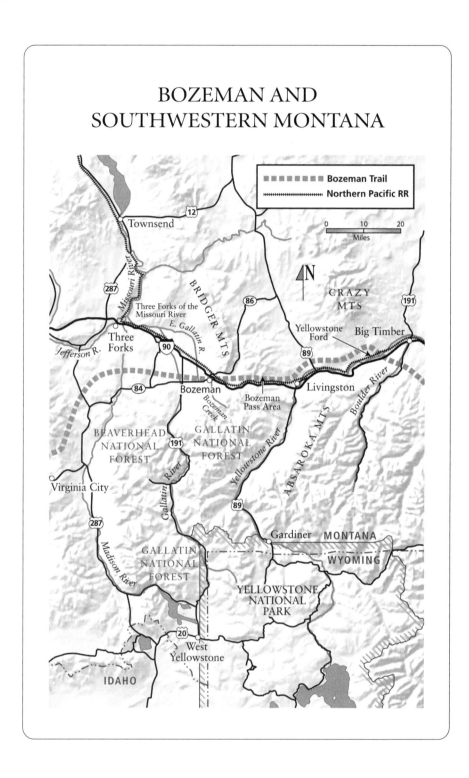

Bozeman Trail
Northern Pacific RR

0   10   20
Miles

N

Townsend

CRAZY
MTS

Three Forks of the
Missouri River

Yellowstone
Ford

Big Timber

E. Gallatin R.

Three
Forks

Jefferson R.

BRIDGER MTS

Bozeman

Bozeman
Pass Area

Livingston

Bozeman
Creek

BEAVERHEAD
NATIONAL
FOREST

GALLATIN
NATIONAL
FOREST

ABSAROKA MTS

Boulder River

Yellowstone River

Virginia City

Gallatin River

Gardiner   MONTANA

WYOMING

GALLATIN
NATIONAL
FOREST

Madison River

YELLOWSTONE
NATIONAL
PARK

West
Yellowstone

IDAHO

Missouri River

PLAINS, PLOWS, AND PEAS

I see in retrospect the growth and development of a small western town; a rich mountain valley. Through the rigors of winter, through the buoyant hopes of summer, through the toil of endless days a vigorous people left homes and civilization, willing to brave the hardships and dangers in a new and undeveloped country. They deserve recognition; we are enjoying the fruits of their labor.
—FRED WILLSON

ONE HUNDRED MILLION YEARS AGO, a shallow inland sea covered the Gallatin Valley; about sixty million years ago, massive upheavals began forming today's Rocky Mountains. Volcanic activity accompanied the mountain building, producing the dust that later became rich soil. This soil covers much of the valley today and is the basis for its agricultural success.

A jagged semicircle of mountains defines the Gallatin Valley, and it is these high peaks that capture what is the area's most important natural resource: water. Snowmelt runoff creates the creeks and rivers that crisscross the valley, notably the East Gallatin River, which meanders through the northeast portion of Bozeman. Other creeks include Bozeman (or Sourdough)

For centuries, the Madison Buffalo Jump west of Bozeman provided prehistoric people with food, clothing, and tools. The use of buffalo jumps ended during the eighteenth century as tribes obtained horses. AUTHOR

Creek, which flows from the Gallatin Range through the city and into the East Gallatin River; Nash Spring and Matthew Bird creeks, which cross through the southern portion of Bozeman; Middle Creek, which passes to Bozeman's southwest; Mill Creek and Rocky Creek, which flow into the northeast section of Bozeman; and Bridger Creek, which empties out of the Bridger Range to join Bozeman and Rocky creeks to form the East Gallatin. West of Bozeman sits what might be considered the historic epicenter of the Gallatin Valley—the Three Forks of the Missouri River. Overall, some 250 creeks wind through Gallatin County, and this, when taken with the valley's vast supply of groundwater, means that Bozeman is surrounded by water. That resource brought people to the valley thousands of years ago and still provides the basis for the area's development.

Peopling the Gallatin Valley

NO ONE KNOWS WHEN THE FIRST PEOPLE came to the Gallatin Valley. Archaeologists have found evidence that demonstrates human habitation at least as far back as five thousand years ago, while evidence from other locations in southwestern Montana dates from the Clovis Period, over eleven thousand years ago. Early humans left their mark on the land: tipi rings and pictographs testify to their use of the valley's grasslands, the Bridger Range, and the Gallatin Canyon.

By the early Archaic Period, beginning about 5000 B.C., the region's early residents had become increasingly sophisticated hunters and gatherers. Throughout today's landscape, archaeologists have found projectile points used for hunting and basin-shaped milling stones and other tools used for processing plants. The Gallatin Valley was an important place for communal hunts and the seasonal gathering of a variety of plants.

A significant reminder of the lives of Montana's early people exists at the Madison Buffalo Jump, twenty-three miles west of Bozeman. The bison herds that roamed the Gallatin Valley represented a vast supply source, and tribal people took advantage of the fortuitous location of a bison trail near the peak of the plateau. Hunters built drive lines, which diverted the bison from the trail over the edge of the cliff. The charging bison fell more than fifty feet and tumbled several hundred

Tribal encampments were a common feature around Bozeman and the Gallatin Valley into the 1870s. Early diarists told of trading with tribal people who were passing through town on their way to seasonal hunting grounds. Crow lodges are shown in this circa 1875 photograph. PIONEER MUSEUM

yards down the steep slope below the cliff in a dramatic scene of dust, noise, and death. Archaeologists have uncovered an extensive bone deposit from over two thousand years ago, as well as associated features such as food-processing sites, tipi rings, and eagle-catching pits that demonstrate intensive use of the area. The jump remained in active use until approximately 1800 A.D., when horses, new trade goods, and disease transformed traditional patterns throughout the plains.

Even before the introduction of the horse, the region's residents were highly mobile; dogs were important beasts of burden and hunting assistants. At some Gallatin Valley sites, archaeologists have found projectile points made of obsidian from ancient quarries in Yellowstone National Park, demonstrating supply and trade networks and the migratory treks they inspired. These cultural remains reflect traditions and social patterns in the same way that architecture often reflects our own life patterns and customs.

Between 500 and 1700 A.D., the tribal groups we know today probably first organized, with larger tribes reaching populations as high as several thousand individuals. These large groups did not live together. Instead, each tribe was composed of a number of bands that included several extended families. Members of a band traveled together on their seasonal rounds. This travel to specific places at certain times to hunt, fish, or meet with other bands provided people with a rhythm to their year and linked tribal people to the land through familiar, traditional cycles.

In the 1800s, horses, guns, and disease transformed the lives of Montana's tribal people. On horseback, Plains Indians became increasingly efficient hunters. They could travel longer distances, and their increased mobility intensified territorial disputes with neighboring tribes. Firearms, of course, made their encounters more dangerous. Among those traversing the rich hunting grounds of the Gallatin Valley were the Salish, Blackfeet, Crows, Nez Perce, and Shoshones.

Far more dangerous than enemy tribes, however, were new diseases to which Indians had little resistance—the most disastrous legacy of European and American exploration and settlement. One anthropologist has estimated that the wave of regional epidemics may have begun with a smallpox epidemic in the 1770s. Prior to this, for example, the Salish population stood at about 15,000. By the time Meriwether Lewis and William Clark first encountered the Salish in September 1805, the tribe's population hovered between 2,700 and 5,500. Weakened by disease, the tribes were in no condition to successfully negotiate when Euro-American settlers finally arrived in the territory en masse.

The Lewis and Clark Expedition was the vanguard of a new age of settlement in the American West. Upon arrival at the Three Forks of the Missouri River, Lewis observed, "There is timber enough here to support an establishment, provided

In Lewis and Clark at the Three Forks *(1912), painter Edward S. Paxson fancifully imagined the moment that Sacagawea recognized the Three Forks of the Missouri, an important hunting ground used by her tribe, the Lemhi Shoshone, and the spot where she had been kidnapped by members of the Mandan tribe.* MHS

it be erected with brick or stone either of which would be much cheaper than wood as all the materials for such a work are immediately at the spot." The conditions for farming and grazing, he concluded, were "much in favor of an establishment should it ever be thought necessary to fix one at this place."

The expedition's return journey brought Clark even closer to today's Bozeman. As his party traveled through the Gallatin Valley, he noted in his journal the profusion of game—an

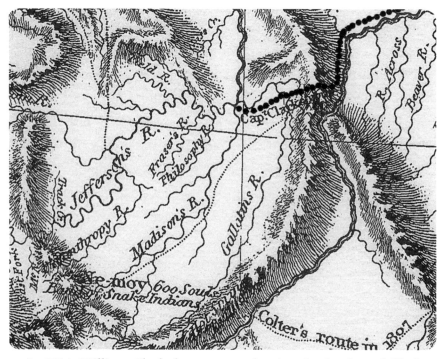

In 1814, William Clark drew a map charting the Lewis and Clark Expedition's route through the American West, which was published as part of the first official account of the expedition, History of the Expedition under the Command of Captains Lewis and Clark. *A dotted line on this detail from Clark's map shows the route through the "gap in the mountain," today's Bozeman Pass.*

observation that soon attracted fur trappers to Montana's beaver-rich streams. Clark also paid due respect to Sacagawea: "The indian woman who has been of Great service to me as a pilot through this country recommends a gap in the mountains more south which I shall cross." This "gap in the mountains"— known today as Bozeman Pass—would prove critical to the formation of Bozeman.

Lewis and Clark proved an inspiration to fur trappers and fur-trading companies seeking to locate new markets and new resources. In fact, on their voyage home, some members of the expedition reversed course, choosing to seek their fortune in the fur trade. Prominent among these was John Colter, who, with permission from the two captains, left the expedition to join trappers heading back up the Missouri.

During the next several years, trappers did their best to exploit the resources of the Gallatin Valley, despite fierce resistance from some tribes, most prominently the Blackfeet. The fur business lasted until the late 1830s, when the market collapsed because stylish Europeans began to favor silk over beaver pelts for men's hats. Euro-American settlers had little other reason to travel to Montana, even after miners struck gold in California in 1848. Too distant from established roads and commercial centers, the Gallatin Valley would not see permanent Euro-American settlement until the 1860s.

Transforming the Land

"IF HELL LAY TO THE WEST," went a nineteenth-century saying, "Americans would cross heaven to get there." It must have seemed that way to those who witnessed the stampede westward to the newly discovered goldfields, first in California, then in Colorado, and finally in Idaho and Montana. Rumors of gold in Montana had circulated for years. Gold was first discovered at what became Gold Creek in the mid-1850s, but it was the first major strike at Bannack in summer 1862 that drew the legions of treasure seekers to the territory.

In 1863, prospecting parties began to push farther into southwestern Montana. In one instance, a few men split off from a larger group, and, in an effort to avoid a Crow war party, they found themselves camping along a lonely creek. The men had stumbled into one of the wealthiest goldfields in the region. Legend has it that one of the men struck gold when he dug a plate into the creek hoping only to glean enough "color" for tobacco money.

By the end of 1863, some six thousand miners were crowded along the narrow waterway called Alder Creek, near Virginia City. More strikes followed—including one at Last Chance Gulch, in present-day Helena—and with each new find, the territory increased in both population and wealth. But some of Montana's new settlers sought a new start away from the hard life at the diggings. For one such group, the Three Forks beckoned. There the men found land perfectly suited for raising crops and livestock, and they seized the opportunity to make money by selling these goods to nearby miners. Dubbed Gallatin City, the town, one of the first settlements in Montana, was laid out in late 1862. Although it became the original seat of government for Gallatin County, the community soon found itself eclipsed by a new settlement, thirty-one miles to the southeast, along the Bozeman Trail.

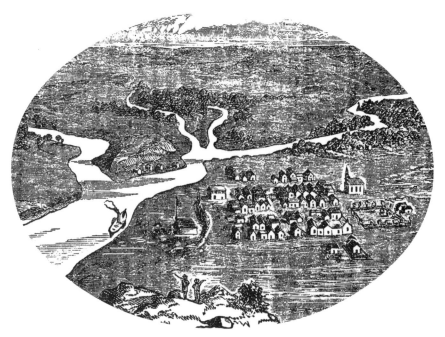

*Produced as part of an effort to promote immigration to Montana
Territory, this 1864 rendering depicts an idealized Gallatin City. From
1862 to 1863, the first Gallatin City occupied the west bank of the
Missouri River near the Three Forks. When that settlement struggled to
survive, a second Gallatin City was established across the river. Despite
being named the first seat of Gallatin County in 1865, Gallatin City
faded as Bozeman grew, all but disappearing when the Northern Pacific
Railroad bypassed it in 1883.* MHS

That trail, and ultimately the town, was named for John
Bozeman, an occasional farmer and miner who left his family
in Georgia in 1860 to seek opportunity in the West. After an
unsuccessful attempt at gold mining, Bozeman turned to guiding, and in 1863, with partner John M. Jacobs, he scouted a
shortcut from the Platte River Road to the new Montana goldfields. The trail was both dangerous and illegal, since it
trespassed on land reserved for the tribes under the Fort

Laramie Treaty of 1851. Nevertheless, Congress funded improvements to the route, and perhaps as many as thirty-five hundred people traveled along the Bozeman Trail before Indian resistance in the form of Red Cloud's War forced its permanent closure in 1866.

The trail entered the Gallatin Valley over the Bozeman Pass, and almost all of the emigrants who kept travel diaries described the euphoria they felt when Bozeman—then just a small collection of cabins—came into view. Davis Willson described his train's arrival in 1866:

> [We] soon came to the summit of a hill from which we could see stretching far away before us the Gallatin Valley. Beautiful Valley. All took off our hats and swung them. . . . The first thing we saw that showed signs of a settlement & gave us the smile of civilization was a fence! At this we cheered vociferously! On a little farther and saw a ranch! Another cheer! More ranches, more cheers! . . . And once for all a cheer for the whole country and our safe arrival!

John Bozeman's tenure as a guide was brief, but he converted his status as a celebrity into publicity for the town he founded in 1864 with two friends, Daniel Rouse and William Beall. They situated the settlement, originally called Jacobs' Crossing after Bozeman's partner, "right in the gate of the mountains." As Bozeman famously noted, they chose their site "ready to swallow up all the tenderfeet that would reach the territory from the east, with their golden fleeces to be taken care of."

By summer 1864, Rouse had erected the community's first log cabin while Beall took out a claim half a mile west and north of the corner of today's Main Street and Bozeman

Knowing there was money to be made in finding a shorter route from the Midwest to the Montana goldfields, John Bozeman (left, circa 1860) located the route that became known as the Bozeman Trail. Emigrants who wanted to reach the diggings as fast as possible were willing to pay guides such as Bozeman high rates to escort them to the territory.
Pioneer Museum

Avenue. The Reverend William W. Alderson, William Tracy, and others soon took up claims nearby, and on August 9, 1864, the tiny village's twelve founders officially met as the Upper East Gallatin Society. Together, they named their new community Bozeman and laid out preliminary boundaries to establish the township, though the official U.S. government land survey would not be completed until 1867.

Thomas Jefferson would have found his dream of an agrarian-based America alive in the early Gallatin Valley, which, according to Bozeman, was "being fast settled up with farmers, many of whom came to Montana as a better class of miners." By the mid-1860s, the first crops were harvested, with wheat, potatoes, grains, and vegetables finding markets in regional mining communities.

Although the valley was blessed with ready water and rich soil, settlers still faced unpredictable weather and limited access to markets during those early days—two problems that the enthusiastic Meriwether Lewis had failed to foresee. The fickle weather must have puzzled early settlers, many of whom had come from states with longer growing seasons and more predictable frosts. In 1865, William W. Alderson recorded his frustration in his diary: "Frequent showers of snow and such

In 1865, early Bozeman entrepreneurs William and Perry McAdow and partner Tom Cover wasted no time constructing the township's first commercial flour and gristmill, shown here in this undated photograph. The mill was located three blocks from the town site. MHS

hard freezing at nights occur that it is really discouraging to a person expecting to make money farming here." In 1883, his son Matthew echoed the sentiment, writing, "Montana is a poor place for drones. A man to withstand the rigors of any northern climate must have at least the courage at heart to brave almost anything and fight his way through." Despite these complaints, the Aldersons and others like them persevered to make a profit and build a town.

In 1865, about twenty thousand bushels of wheat were produced on about fifteen hundred tilled acres in the Gallatin Valley. Soon, irrigation ditches began to zigzag across the valley, increasing the amount of arable land. Brothers Merritt and Oscar Penwell dug the earliest known irrigation ditch, in 1864, to bring water from the East Gallatin River to their fields. Following the Penwells' example, other farmers pooled their resources to construct ditches and small-scale canals. The early 1870s also saw the region's first large-scale irrigation project with the diversion of water from the West Gallatin River into Middle Creek, the channel dug collectively by the farmers who formed the Upper Middle Creek Ditch Company.

To mill the wheat harvested by the Gallatin Valley's growing number of farmers, brothers William and Perry McAdow and partner Tom Cover built a flour mill in 1865. Located just east of Bozeman, the mill could produce one thousand sacks of flour per week. Soon, other new mills were being built. In 1867, the Penwell brothers' water-powered Union Flour Mill was born. In 1878, George Thomas relocated a Gallatin City mill to Springhill, the small community that still stands today eight miles north of Bozeman, nestled against the foothills of

A resourceful businessman, Nelson Story, pictured here circa 1880, parlayed the money he made in the Virginia City goldfields into a commercial empire based in Bozeman. MOR

the Bridger Mountains. Thomas brought a new technology to Montana milling that made it possible to manufacture white flour, similar to that produced today.

Cattle and dairy operations also made an early economic impact on the Gallatin Valley, thanks largely to entrepreneur Nelson Story. By 1866, the twenty-eight-year-old Story had made his fortune in the Alder Gulch diggings. He then took thirty thousand dollars in gold dust to New York City, and, capitalizing on the high price of bullion during the Civil War era, he traded the gold for forty thousand dollars in greenbacks. He took those greenbacks to Texas, where he bought longhorns and hired cowboys to drive them north. His cattle drive ended in the upper Yellowstone Valley, near present-day Livingston.

Later, Story—now a living legend thanks to the cattle drive—relocated a Salesville (now Gallatin Gateway) mill to the mouth of Bridger Canyon. The improved complex, known as Story Mill (**sites 39–42**), could produce up to 100 bushels of flour per day. Following a devastating 1901 fire, Story rebuilt his mill. He soon acquired the nearby Farmers Mill, building a thriving business with a milling capacity of 650 bushels per day. Story Mill produced an immense fortune for Story over the coming decades.

In the 1860s, however, Bozeman's destiny remained dependent upon uncertain transportation and supply routes and the boom-and-bust economies of neighboring mining camps. The future was anything but assured. Then, in spring 1867, John Bozeman was murdered on the Yellowstone River, where he had traveled with partner Tom Cover to establish a ferry and toll bridge. While this mystery will probably never be solved, many believe Cover murdered Bozeman. At the time, though, Cover convincingly blamed a Blackfeet war party—a story many settlers were predisposed to believe.

Bozeman's death created panic, and, frightened of meeting the same fate as the town founder, Gallatin Valley residents prepared to meet an attack and appealed to the federal and territorial governments for military protection. Their pleas for protection netted a much-hoped-for military post. In August 1867, the U.S. Army established Fort Ellis just east of Bozeman. The fort proved critical to Bozeman's economic future while offering the defense settlers believed they needed.

Originally, Fort Ellis was an infantry post. Eventually, the army saw the folly of protecting settlers from mounted Indian

This late 1870s photo shows citizens reviewing Fort Ellis troopers. Fort commanders contracted with local entrepreneurs for supplies, providing early commercial security for the Gallatin Valley. MHS

attacks with foot soldiers and in 1869 supplemented the post with two cavalry companies. In all, five companies were posted to Fort Ellis, and while each company was rarely at full strength, there were probably two hundred to three hundred men stationed at the fort at any given time.

Soldiers at Fort Ellis took part in two emblematic events in Montana's frontier history. The first was the Marias, or Baker, Massacre. Led by Major Eugene Baker, Fort Ellis troopers headed north in January 1870 in search of Mountain Chief's band of Blackfeet. Their mission was to apprehend two men thought responsible for the murder of a trader. They attacked the first village they came upon, the winter camp of the Blackfeet leader Heavy Runner, whose people had no connection to the murder of the trader. Most of the warriors were away when the troops ambushed the village at dawn. What followed, according to one army participant, was "the greatest slaughter of Indians ever made by U.S. troops." Over 150 people died in the attack, and many more froze to death as they struggled to reach Fort Shaw, near Helena, in the bitter cold.

The second event was the celebrated 1871 expedition to explore the upper Yellowstone Valley led by geologist Ferdinand V. Hayden. Fort Ellis troops escorted Hayden and his team of scientists, artists, and topographers through the heart of Yellowstone country, stopping at Mammoth Hot Springs before continuing along the Lamar River. Photographer William Henry Jackson and artist Thomas Moran accompanied the expedition, and their stunning images of the area helped persuade Congress to designate it as the country's first national park in 1872. Park tourism slowly flourished thereafter, a happy development for Bozeman business interests who had worked hard to promote the national park idea.

The fort and its soldiers had a more immediate effect on the Bozeman economy, offering economic stability to the young town by providing a critical market for Gallatin Valley farmers and merchants. The fort's several hundred men and horses needed constant supply. The Crow Agency, then located to the east on the Yellowstone River, provided another market of significant size.

The role of Fort Ellis and the Crow Agency in Bozeman's economy points to a larger truth about the region's development. For all the pioneering spirit and individual initiative shown by the Gallatin Valley's early settlers, much of the community's nineteenth-century success was directly linked

Classes met in Bozeman's first brick school, the West Side School, for only fourteen years before the crumbling edifice was demolished. The school is pictured here during construction in 1877. MOR

to the federal government's policy: its military presence, its encouragement of westward migration through the 1862 Homestead Act, and its massive investment in railroad construction. Government policy and eastern capital made the hard-won successes of individual settlers possible.

By the early 1870s, new Main Street buildings reflected the valley's growing commercial and agricultural success. The emigrants whose wagon trains wound their way through Montana found respite in Main Street hotels: first at the hewn-log, one-and-one-half-story Stafford-Rice Hotel; then at the wood-framed, two-story Guy House; and finally at the 1867 Metropolitan Hotel, built with bricks imported from Helena.

As the town grew, so did its civic and architectural sophistication. Schools were established in Bozeman soon after the first families arrived over Bozeman Pass in the 1860s. A local tax provided funding for public education in 1868; not long after, William Beall built the community's first frame schoolhouse. Beall also designed Bozeman's first large-scale school, constructed in 1877. Known as the West Side School, this brick, five-room schoolhouse—located on what is today the grounds of the Emerson Center for the Arts and Culture— was replaced with a new building in 1892; a local newspaper described the new West Side School as adding "to the architectural beauty and substantiability [*sic*] of Bozeman's appearance." In 1883, Bozeman built the brick, two-story East Side School at 114 North Rouse Avenue, where today's Hawthorne School (**site 48**) now stands.

The late 1860s saw Bozeman's first newspaper, the *Pick and the Plow,* which began printing on December 31, 1869. The *Pick and the Plow* had a short life, and the *Bozeman Times* began publication in the 1870s. It was the Republican-influenced *Bozeman Avant-Courier,* however, which began circulation in 1871, that remained a fixture in the community, often exchanging editorial broadsides with the Democratic *Bozeman Chronicle,* which began publishing in January 1883.

Despite the town's growing wealth, it could not escape the effects of a nationwide depression, the Panic of 1873. The collapse of overextended banking and railroading industries nationwide triggered the economic catastrophe, which led to widespread unemployment. The New York Stock Exchange closed, and the United States entered a five-year depression, during which the country was plagued by high unemployment, wage cuts, strikes, factory closures, and falling agricultural prices. Banks failed, including Bozeman's original First National Bank, which closed its doors in 1878. In Bozeman, as in the rest of the country, growth slowed to a standstill.

In 1874, town leaders decided to take action to ensure the community's future. They sponsored an expedition of 146 men to establish new roads along the Yellowstone River, locate new town sites, and investigate rumors of mineral wealth as far east as the Powder and Tongue rivers. Intended to revive the local economy, the Yellowstone Expedition drew the wary eyes of Fort Ellis officers, who feared that such an incursion into tribal hunting grounds recognized by the 1868 Treaty of Fort Laramie would start a new war.

The expedition departed Bozeman on a freezing February day and reached Rosebud Creek east of present-day Billings in May before deciding to return to Bozeman. Though expedition members did improve the existing Yellowstone Road, they established no new roads, mines, or towns. Nor did they ignite a new war, despite some bloody skirmishes with the Sioux. Just two years later, however, the Great Sioux War of 1876–77 began, a conflict in which Fort Ellis troopers participated. Despite tribal victories at Rosebud Creek and the Little Bighorn, the U.S. Army defeated the Lakota Sioux and Northern Cheyennes. With this defeat, warfare on Montana's open plains largely came to an end, as did the need for many frontier military outposts throughout the West.

The Iron Horse and the 1880s

FOR BOZEMAN, one of the most drastic consequences of the depression of the 1870s was the delayed arrival of the Northern Pacific Railroad. The Northern Pacific surveyed a route across Bozeman Pass in 1872, and according to surveyor, businessman, and local booster Peter Koch, "we all believed that the time had come when our front door was to be swung wide open. But again we were doomed to disappointment." Financial problems brought the railroad's progress to a halt in 1873.

By early 1882, the financially restored Northern Pacific was

Whether or not a railroad chose to route its line through a particular town often meant the difference between that town becoming a thriving commercial center or a ghost town. True to this pattern, the Northern Pacific brought prosperity to Bozeman in 1883. In 1892, as part of an improvement campaign undertaken in an effort to secure the state capital for Bozeman, the original passenger depot was rebuilt as the more substantial brick building seen on the left in this undated photograph **(site 36).** PIONEER MUSEUM once again holding out the promise of prosperity to Bozeman—but if only its route came through the town. At the time, the Northern Pacific was busily surveying other possible routes closer to Yellowstone National Park. To win the railroad, community leaders engaged in an aggressive campaign to convince railroad officials that Bozeman was the right choice. They succeeded, and on March 21, 1883, the community officially greeted the first Northern Pacific train as it pulled into a simple wood-frame depot located northeast of Main Street on land donated by the McAdow family. The small depot and rail yard along the Northern Pacific's main line sparked the growth of what became known as Bozeman's northeast neighborhood, long the town's most eclectic area.

The eagerly anticipated arrival of the railroad confirmed the high hopes many locals had for their town. The city incorporated in 1883 and elected its first city commission. Bozeman had been growing prior to the railroad's arrival, but the iron horse increased commercial and residential development. Local brick manufacturers had trouble meeting demand as developers built new business blocks to house the banks, butcher shops, saloons, drug stores, cigar factories, and dress shops that lined the expanding Main Street. Bozeman had begun its transformation from a frontier village to a thriving town.

Continued growth brought its own problems, however, and established residents soon complained about the transients brought to town by the railroad. Among the ways local leaders sought to control the wandering poor was a law that made vagrancy a misdemeanor. The law defined vagrants as "healthy beggars who solicit alms," "every idler and dissolute person or

One of two local brickyards in the early 1880s, the Lewis and Carey Brickyard, located about a mile south of Main Street, manufactured its products out of clay taken from the banks of Bozeman Creek. From Michael Leeson, History of Montana, 1735–1885 *(Chicago, 1885).*

associate of known thieves," or a "dissolute person who lives in and about houses of ill fame." This statute, remarkable for its nineteenth-century language, is still on Bozeman's books.

The editors of the *Avant-Courier* advocated even harsher measures to minimize vagrancy. The newspaper championed a vigilante movement, stating that "Tramps and roughs are getting too numerous in and around Bozeman. [We are] in favor of following the example of Butte in making the 3-7-77 [a symbol of Montana vigilante movements] an omen to be feared. We are informed that the organization in our town is fully equipped and that it includes no less than 150 brave, old-time citizens."

A far more real danger for agriculturally dependent Bozeman was Montana's notorious climate. During the "hard winter" of 1886–87, extreme cold and heavy snows combined to bring the deaths of an estimated 362,000 head of cattle—60 percent of Montana's total. In eastern Montana, estimated losses reached as high as 95 percent. Among the Gallatin Valley ranchers who suffered the effects of the hard winter was Nelson Story, who lost over 66 percent of his stock. The next season, Story divested his cattle interests, selling approximately 13,000 head of cattle in what was then one of the largest livestock transactions in the history of western ranching.

Fortunately for Bozeman, a political development—Montana's graduation from territory to state in 1889—spurred another wave of development. Determined to claim the new state capital for their town, local promoters vied against six other communities for the honor of claiming the capital, and the fierce competition resulted in some notable Bozeman buildings. George Hancock, a respected North Dakota architect, designed both the beautiful stone Gothic Revival–style St. James Episcopal Church at 5 West Olive Street (**site 63**) and the Bozeman Hotel at 321 East Main Street (**site 23**). The town's most expensive and largest commercial structure to date, the hotel, which cost over one hundred thousand dollars to build, opened to great fanfare in 1891.

Architect Byron Vreeland made his own splash just across the street from the Bozeman Hotel. Hailed as a grand achievement, his 1890 Bozeman City Hall and Opera House symbolized all that Bozeman promoters hoped to accomplish by landing the capital. Its flamboyant Second Empire–style

Observers described the City Hall and Opera House on East Main Street (pictured here in the 1890s) as the grandest opera house between Butte, Montana, and Fargo, North Dakota. The building was used as city offices until the city demolished it as part of the Urban Renewal program in 1966. PIONEER MUSEUM

adornment and massive size offered an unmatched display of wealth and power. Vreeland also chose the Second Empire style, a style embraced by the Gilded Age's industrial giants, for the palatial residence built by Nelson Story in 1888. With the completion of the home, Vreeland's buildings capped Main Street—his Story Mansion and the original Gallatin County Courthouse marked the west end of Main, while the Bozeman City Hall and Opera House at the eastern end welcomed those who arrived over the Bozeman Pass by wagon, horseback, or train. A new brick mercantile with a stylish Moorish turret, the 1889 Tilton Building, occupied the northeast corner of Rouse Avenue and Main Street, making the intersection Bozeman's architectural hub.

Another concern for Bozeman residents as they contemplated becoming the state capital was schools. By the late 1880s, the need for a high school was apparent, but it was difficult for a small town like Bozeman to support secondary education. In recognition of this statewide problem, the Montana legislature passed the County Free High School Act, allowing counties to create countywide high school districts. Despite this measure, however, it was not until 1902 that Gallatin County built the Gallatin County High School at 404 West Main Street (today's Willson School, **site 3**). Today, that building still casts its formidable architectural shadow over Main Street.

As the statewide referendum to decide the state capital grew closer, Bozeman developers continued their efforts to win the capital. To the south of Main Street, they confidently platted the Capitol Hill Addition and South Eighth Avenue, which connected the new addition to Main Street. Although no one lived in the development and no construction actually occurred, anyone looking at a map of Bozeman was sure to be impressed by the city's transformation. The changes to Bozeman also included construction of a local transportation system. Tracks for the electrified streetcar system were laid in spring 1892. On July 27, 1892, still months before the capital question would be decided at the ballot box, three new streetcars traveled a route that took them west from the

The Gallatin Light, Power, and Railway Company founded Bozeman's streetcar system, which used electricity generated by a nearby creek to power the streetcars. Here, a trolley rattles along North Church Street during the late 1890s. PIONEER MUSEUM

new brick Northern Pacific depot (**site 36**, another result of capital fever), then south on Church Avenue and west on Main Street, then south again to what many optimistically believed would be the grand entrance to the new capitol building at the southern end of the Capital Hill Addition.

Despite these efforts and other schemes, Bozeman placed a disappointing fourth in the 1892 statewide referendum to choose the capital city. The following year, however, Bozeman received a consolation prize when the state legslature—responding in part to lobbying by State Board of Education member Nelson Story—chose the town as the site of the Agricultural

College of the State of Montana, popularly known as the Montana Agricultural College, and the new State Agricultural Experiment Station.

A furious debate ensued over where to situate the new college, but ultimately the chairman of the local board of education, Peter Koch, selected the site, which was at the time the county poor farm. The college and experiment station had to be close to each other, he argued, and there was a dearth of unallocated water closer to Main Street. The poor farm held a water right and was relatively close to the commercial district, whose business interests wanted the new pool of customers as nearby as possible.

The awarding of the college could not have come at a more critical time. The economic bubble that had sustained Bozeman

*Completed in 1896, Montana Hall (**site 145**, left), historically called Old Main, was one of the first two buildings built on the new campus of the Montana Agricultural College. The other two buildings in this pre-1920 photograph, the Chemistry Building (middle) and the Gymnasium and Armory (right), were demolished to make room for campus improvements such as the 1923 Lewis Hall.* PIONEER MUSEUM

for over a decade finally burst with the arrival of a disastrous national depression known as the Panic of 1893, one of the most catastrophic economic disintegrations in American history. Nationally, over six hundred banks failed, and three times as many businesses closed as had during the 1873 panic. By 1894, the national unemployment rate was over 18 percent, and farmers, as in the 1870s, were struck hard by falling prices.

Seeking to shore up economic confidence, the *Avant-Courier* buoyantly reported that "the financial depression cannot, in the very nature of things, last very long, nor the hard times prove extremely serious in such a magnificent agricultural county as Gallatin and in a state of such wonderful resources as Montana." While few shared the *Avant-Courier*'s optimism, Bozeman suffered less than other Montana communities, with the new college providing a semblance of economic stability.

Bozeman's New Century

THE STABILITY PROVIDED BY THE COLLEGE and a national economic recovery by the late 1890s meant good times for Bozeman in the new century. In 1900, the town's population stood at 3,419 citizens. The growth of white-collar jobs for civil servants, bankers, real estate developers, and college faculty and administrators fueled an increase in the size and power of the local middle class. Many of these middle-class residents joined civic organizations, including women's clubs and an empowered Women's Christian Temperance Union, which had a vocal and politically active membership in Bozeman.

These organizations took a dim view of Bozeman's seedier aspects. "Female boardinghouses" was one euphemism for houses of prostitution, and a 1904 map of Bozeman shows seven such places on a single block between North Rouse and North Bozeman avenues. This area, Bozeman's red-light district, was also home to opium dens, whose presence contributed to a growing sense of resentment toward the Chinese, even though the vast majority of Chinese residents were not opium abusers had been but former railroad workers who had invested their savings in Main Street laundries and restaurants.

In the earlier Victorian Era, vice had been tolerated, though townspeople sought to confine indecency to its own quarter— hence the creation of red-light districts. By the Progressive Era of the early twentieth century, however, citizens were no longer so accepting. Like their counterparts elsewhere, Bozeman residents looked for ways to clean up their town's most disreputable area. One answer was the 1904 construction of the Carnegie Library at 35 North Bozeman Avenue (**site 28**), which was purposely located directly across the street from the red-light district in the hopes of reclaiming the neighborhood for respectability.

The forces of progress also saw to the construction of new schools, including the original two-story, brick Longfellow School, built in 1905 on South Tracy Avenue complete with a rooftop bell tower. In the continuing effort to honor America's literary giants, the East Side School on North Rouse Avenue was renamed Hawthorne School. On the heels of World War I, architect Fred Willson designed a new school, the Emerson Junior High School, at 111 South Grand Avenue, one block south of the high school (on the same block as the West Side School, which was renamed Irving School). Willson's Gothic-inspired gem drew acclaim for its design. Today the building (**site 64**) serves as the Emerson Center for the Arts and Culture.

Residential neighborhoods grew, too—filled with homes whose designs reflected Progressive Era ideology. For domestic architecture, efficiency became the watchword as social scientists preached the advantages of clean lines and scientific housekeeping—not just for a family's own health but also for the social and political health of the nation. The expectations were perhaps more than any architectural design could bear; nevertheless, they left their mark as contractors constructed blocks of Craftsman- and Colonial Revival–style residences—both stylistically much less ornate than the ostentatious Victorians of a few decades before.

It was during this era that architect Fred Fielding Willson began a career that would span over fifty years and profoundly shape Bozeman. Born in 1877, the son of Bozeman pioneers, Willson attended local schools before entering the Montana Agricultural College. He left Montana to attend New York's Columbia University, graduating with a degree in architecture at age twenty-four. Willson next entered a course of study at the École des Beaux-Arts in Paris. The term "Beaux-Arts style" continues to reflect the influence the school had on a generation of American architects.

Willson returned to the United States to apprentice with architectural firms in the East before returning to the Butte office of the noted Montana architectural firm Link and Haire. Those early days were not easy, and Willson's diary entries

No architect influenced Bozeman more than Fred Fielding Willson, who designed an extraordinary number of commercial, academic, and residential buildings during a career that spanned nearly half a century. He is shown here circa 1930. PIONEER MUSEUM

reflect his frustration. In 1909, he confided in his diary that he "should like to forget about buildings" and that he was "ready to quit." But his work at the Montana Agricultural College with the 1910 design of Hamilton Hall (**site 144**) was a turning point. Shortly thereafter, he left Link and Haire to establish his own practice. Other early Willson buildings include the county jail at 317 West Main Street (**site 1**), now the home of the Gallatin Historical Society and Pioneer Museum.

*Not all of architect Fred Willson's projects went smoothly. Contractors constructed the Willson-designed county jail at 317 West Main Street (**site 1**) in summer 1911. That December, Willson wrote in his diary: "[M]en broke out of new jail. Am being joked plenty."* AUTHOR

Matching the growth of the town was that of the valley, spurred on by the arrival of the Chicago, Milwaukee & St. Paul Railroad (better known as the Milwaukee Road) in 1911. This new rail line provided farmers with competitive rates and greater access to markets. Living close to the State Agricultural Experiment Station provided local farmers with other advantages. A 1914 federal program funded agricultural Extension Service offices in every state, with the goal of increasing farm production and improving rural life. Although each Montana county ultimately had its own Extension officer, the experiment station, based in Taylor Hall (**site 149**), served

Early Bozeman was an island surrounded by seemingly endless wheat fields. In this early 1900s photograph taken looking southwest from the Bridger foothills, the college (left background) is still separated from the residential neighborhoods south of Main Street. MHS

as the program's nerve center. Its proximity allowed Bozeman-area farmers the fastest and most reliable access to a range of services. During this era, experts at the college were involved in livestock-breeding experiments designed to increase the number of animals that could be supported on farms and ranches; the Irrigation Department studied the dryland farming conditions around the state; the Botanical Department was involved in the study and classification of Montana's botanical species; the Chemical Department continued its research into sugar beet production; the Horticultural Department studied ways to adapt fruits and vegetables to Montana's climate; and the station's

Entomology Department examined ways to control the scourge of farmers, the grasshopper.

New crops introduced by the Extension Service had effects beyond increased agricultural efficiency. The experiment station's early-twentieth-century sweet pea trials proved so successful that the valley soon had seventeen thousand acres of the crop in production. Thereafter, canned pea production transformed Bozeman, playing a significant role in the town's social and economic character. In 1916, the Bozeman Canning Company formed, and only ten years later, in its peak year of production, it was packing some 326,000 cases. The unfortunate demands of World War I provided a boon to the local pea industry, and the cannery remained in operation throughout the Great Depression and another world war, finally closing in 1958.

The cannery provided needed jobs for local residents, with men laboring in the fields and women and children working in the factory and seed houses. Young, unmarried women left local farms and moved to town to be closer to the cannery. Female workers often lived together, enjoying a lifestyle far different from a traditional one that emphasized domestic responsibilities. During the Great Depression, women cannery workers helped support their families when unemployed husbands and fathers could not, a situation that enhanced the social and domestic status of many Gallatin Valley women.

During the early decades of the twentieth century, local transportation continued its growth, fueled by rapid population increases. Between 1900 and 1910, Bozeman's population

By the late 1920s, the Gallatin Valley produced 75 percent of the seed peas raised in the United States, and Bozeman became known as the "Sweet Pea Capital of the Nation." This photograph shows the Bozeman Canning Company circa 1950. PIONEER MUSEUM

expanded by over 40 percent while Gallatin County grew by over 65 percent. This surge placed an interurban rail system linking Bozeman to other nearby communities within reach. In 1908, the Gallatin Valley Electric Railway built a new depot on East Main Street and began running cars from Bozeman to Salesville with several stops along the way. One year later, the Chicago, Milwaukee & St. Paul purchased the Bozeman streetcar system and the electric railways as part of its larger goal of constructing a second transcontinental line through the valley. To commemorate the occasion, the village of Salesville changed its name to Gallatin Gateway. Interurban service shut down in 1930, a victim of America's growing car culture.

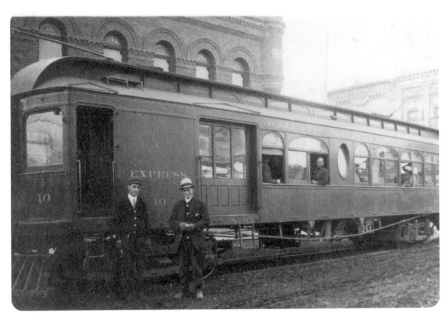

*Interurban #10 pauses in front of the Bozeman Hotel at 321 East Main Street (**site 23**) in this 1910 photo. The streetcar tracks were removed in the late 1930s, but the transportation corridor still functions today as the Galligator Trail.* PIONEER MUSEUM

Meanwhile, the rise of the automobiles had other effects. Since Yellowstone National Park's inception, Bozeman had been the central outfitting point for park-bound tourists— but its role as a tourist community truly boomed after automobiles, rather than railroads, became the transportation choice for tourists. As more automobile tourists visited Bozeman, new building types began to dot the landscape: garages, automobile dealerships, motels, and gas stations. In 1920, Bogert's Grove Tourist Camp, designed especially to accommodate car camping, opened for business. Today, Bogert Park on South Church Avenue (**site 65**) offers a reminder of this early tourism business.

With thriving tourism, agricultural, and transportation industries and an increasingly large and influential college community, Bozeman's potential seemed limitless. During the early decades of the twentieth century, Main Street saw the rise of several new commercial blocks. The 1901 Story Block at 33–39 East Main Street (**site 15**), the 1903 Willson Building at 101 East Main Street (**site 16**), and the impressive 1906 National Bank of Gallatin Valley Building at 1 West Main Street (**site 11**) all testified to the financial security of the thriving town. Bozeman's spiritual centers also began to take new shape,

In 1907, Nelson Story Jr. opened his motor supply store (shown here in an early 1920s photograph) on the northeast corner of Main Street and Grand Avenue. Prior to World War I, the Storys expanded their automotive businesses to include service stations and dealerships on Main Street and North Church and North Wallace Avenues. Pioneer Museum

*Fred Willson designed the Blackmore Apartment Building at 120 South Black Avenue (**site 61**) in 1912 to meet a growing demand for housing. It was Bozeman's first apartment building and boasted the era's most modern conveniences, including electric stoves, iceboxes, and a hot water system powered by the incineration of the tenants' refuse. Investors hoped the U-shaped brick building would attract the young Progressive Era professionals then establishing themselves as part of the town's growing middle class.* AUTHOR

marked, for example, by the 1908 completion of the imposing Holy Rosary Church at 220 West Main Street (**site 4**).

Drought and the crash in commodity prices brought about by the end of World War I had a devastating effect on Montana's economy. However, towns across Montana actually grew as former homesteaders sought new ways to earn their livelihoods. Over 2,500 new arrivals took up residence in Bozeman in the 1920s, increasing the population by nearly one-third. For the first time in the town's history, more people lived in Bozeman than in the rest of Gallatin County—the town now comprised nearly 56 percent of the county's population.

The Great Depression and Beyond

THE ECONOMIC COLLAPSE OF THE 1930S had consequences for locals, but Bozeman survived the Great Depression better than other Montana communities. In contrast to eastern Montana, Bozeman continued to grow, from 6,855 to 8,665 residents during the decade. The drought that gripped much of the West throughout the 1920s finally loosened its hold by the late 1930s, improving prospects in the well-watered and well-irrigated Gallatin Valley. And, as in the past, federal actions proved important in relieving Bozeman's economic distress.

By 1935, New Deal funding through the Works Progress Administration (WPA) was bringing new buildings to the Bozeman cityscape. These federal construction funds had a dual purpose: first and most obviously, to put people to work; and second, to reinvigorate faith in democracy and capitalism. In this time of economic depression and unrest, the government sought to strengthen the links between community and government, a relationship it often represented architecturally.

Bozeman's WPA projects included a new Gallatin County Courthouse at 311 West Main Street (**site 2**) and a new addition to the Gallatin County High School at 404 West Main Street (**site 3**), which resulted in the demolition of Nelson Story's grand old mansion. WPA funds also helped build new buildings designed in the era's popular Streamlined Moderne style for Hawthorne, Longfellow, and Irving schools (**sites 48, 80, and 67**). On South Tracy Avenue, the new Longfellow School replaced the 1905 Colonial Revival–style institution of the same name, while the dated Hawthorne School building on North Rouse Avenue was demolished to make room for a

*One of the many New Deal–era civic buildings devised by Fred Willson, Irving School at 611 South Eighth Avenue (**site 67**) was designed in the Streamlined Moderne style in 1939 and constructed with WPA funding.* AUTHOR

stylish new one. A new Irving School was constructed at a different location, 611 South Eighth Avenue. The guiding hand behind these projects was architect Fred Willson, who embraced the era's new com-mitment to streamlined efficiency.

Just as it created urban work programs, the New Deal addressed the agricultural depression with an alphabet soup of agencies and programs. New Deal nutritional programs provided agricultural processors a much-needed market—a boon for the Montana Flour Mills Company, which thrived on government contracts for cereal, and for the Gallatin Cooperative Creamery, a cooperative established by dairy farmers in 1932 that eventually evolved into Darigold. At the same time, the Extension Service became the center of Montana's New Deal farm policy, and local farms became testing grounds for many Depression Era agricultural initiatives, such as soil conservation programs. The Extension Service's ability to offer solutions to real-world problems enhanced Bozeman's status as the agricultural capital of the state.

New Deal programs waned as the 1930s drew to a close and the nation slowly prepared for another world war. Beginning in 1940, military training programs, such as pilot instruction, began at the college. Architectural change slowed significantly during the 1940s as men, women, and materials were all directed toward the war effort. Not surprisingly, the most notable architectural development of the period was the 1941 construction of the National Guard Armory at 24 West Mendenhall Street (**site 29**).

By the end of the war, vast numbers of returning veterans used federal money designated through the G.I. Bill to attend school and secure loans for homebuilding. In 1945, the college's student population was approximately 1,100 and enrollment increased to almost 5,000 over the next two decades. Faculty numbers increased at a similar rate, growing from 132 to nearly 400. This growth in university attendance—part of the postwar expansion of the middle class—was at the heart of a national economic boom, the largest and most sustained in American history.

While the college expanded, agriculture's economic significance declined in the valley. In 1950, agriculture accounted for nearly 22 percent of all local employment. By 1990, agricultural employment had dropped precipitously to about 3 percent. Bozeman, however, has continued to expand at a tremendous rate, supported in recent decades by an economy based in part on the high-tech, communications,

*The once abandoned Northern Pacific Freight Depot at 611 East Main Street (**site 25**) is now home to Montana Aleworks (above), a popular local gathering place that incorporates into its own logo the Northern Pacific's distinctive red and black monad.* AUTHOR

health, and education sectors. Service and retail industries also form a healthy share of Bozeman's employment and economy. As a result, new subdivisions and commercial spaces are being built on what was once valued farmland. Between 1993 and 1998, over nine thousand acres surrounding Bozeman were subdivided, and pressure on the region's remaining farmland continues.

Even as this development occurs, Bozeman continues to embrace its historic core. Today's East Main Street, for example, has seen a renaissance that began with the resurrection of vacant historic buildings, while new downtown construction has been

*Across the street from the Aleworks stands the restored 1916 Nash-Finch Building (**site 26**). The recent renaissance of East Main Street demonstrates how restored historic buildings can act as foundations for economic growth.* AUTHOR

sensitive to the historic architecture of Bozeman's commercial center. The mounting interest in historic preservation—fueled, in part, by the significance of heritage tourism to Bozeman's economy—has led to a widespread commitment to protect the city's historic neighborhoods. It is these areas we will explore in the next section.

BOZEMAN
HISTORIC DISTRICTS

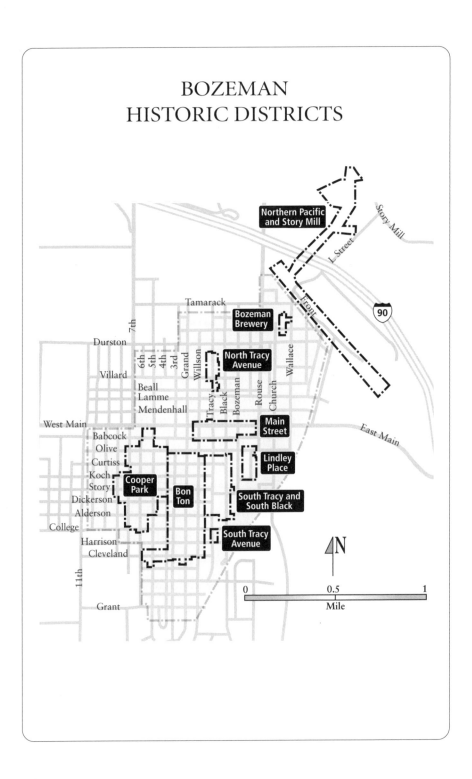

Northern Pacific and Story Mill

Story Mill

L. Street

90

Tamarack

Bozeman Brewery

Front

Durston

7th

North Tracy Avenue

Wallace

6th
5th
4th
3rd
Grand
Willson

Villard

Beall
Lamme
Mendenhall

Tracy
Black
Bozeman
Rouse
Church

West Main

Main Street

East Main

Babcock
Olive
Curtiss
Koch
Story
Dickerson
Alderson
College

Cooper Park

Bon Ton

Lindley Place

South Tracy and South Black

South Tracy Avenue

Harrison
Cleveland

11th

N

Grant

0   0.5   1
Mile

LOOKING AT BOZEMAN'S
HISTORIC BUILDINGS

*Not a fence pole nor a log house was then in sight to designate
the future city of Bozeman. After looking around, however,
for a few moments, we noticed a small wedge tent constructed
out of a wagon cover and after a little careful inspection we
found a lonesome occupant.*
—William W. Alderson

WHEN EIGHTEEN-YEAR-OLD SARAH JANE BESSEY TRACY arrived
in Bozeman in 1869, she confided in her diary that "the whole
prairie south of town seemed covered with Indian teepees." Tracy
was among the first Euro-American women in Bozeman. In the
course of her lifetime, she would witness native people con-
fined to reservations, the arrival of the railroad, and Bozeman's
transformation from an isolated frontier colony to a cosmo-
politan community of farmers, merchants, professionals, and
academics. She would also see Bozeman's Main Street grow from
temporary cabins and log buildings with false fronts to the architectural styles and building forms we recognize today.

Bozeman's earliest residential and commercial core was
concentrated along the Bozeman Trail and surrounded by a
small but growing number of farms and ranches. Early on,

*This circa 1895 image looking west down Main Street shows Bozeman's new urbanity, a result of the campaign to become the state capital. The corner of Main Street and Rouse Avenue appears in the foreground, with the City Hall and Opera House on the left and the Bozeman Hotel (*site 23*) and the Tilton Building on the right.* PIONEER MUSEUM

Main Street served as both the commercial and residential district. Residences and commercial buildings stood snugly side by side. If Main Street lots remained unfilled, it was due to a stagnant economy, not the desire for open space.

Maps provide one way to trace Bozeman's development, and good, detailed maps exist, thanks both to early Bozeman promoters who used bird's-eye views to publicize the community's development and D. A. Sanborn, whose company hired an army of surveyors to map towns across the United States. The bird's-eye views provide artistic aerial views of the town, down to the architectural detailing on some prominent buildings.

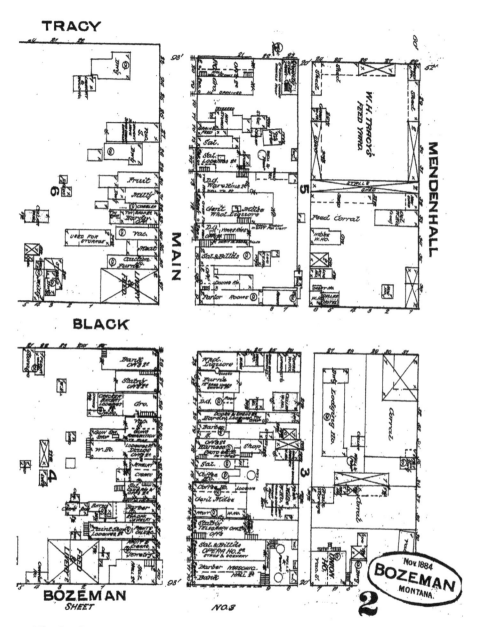

The Sanborn Map Company eventually produced maps of over twelve
thousand cities and towns across the United States. This detail of Main
Street is from the first map the company created for Bozeman in 1884,
twenty years after the town's founding and more than a year after the
arrival of the railroad. MHS

Sanborn maps, on the other hand, were created for use by fire insurance companies so they could assess risk and calculate replacement costs. These detailed, color-coded maps present the city block by block, recording both those structures touted by promoters—schools, mansions, brick business blocks—and those that were not—saloons, cabins, and brothels.

In 1884, two maps—the first Sanborn map of Bozeman and a bird's-eye map—provided the first detailed look of early Bozeman. The Sanborn map concentrates on the commercial core and depicts Main Street between Rouse and Tracy avenues. Much as they do today, diverse businesses—breweries, drug stores, banks, and restaurants—lined Main Street. The buildings' scale and the dominant building materials, however, were dramatically different. Single-story, wood-frame buildings predominated in 1884, with a few multi-storied masonry commercial buildings mixed in, notably the Cooper/Black Building at 118 East Main Street (**site 17**), the Lamme Block at 23–29 East Main Street (**site 14**), and the Spieth and Krug Brewery Building at 240–246 East Main Street (**site 21**). Bozeman Creek still flowed through town, and wooden bridges spanned the creek over Main and Babcock streets.

Before automobiles, and for the sake of frontier-era safety, people wanted to live as close as possible to where they worked and to one another. Single-story, wood-frame residences dotted Main Street east and west of the commercial core. Houses clustered on South Bozeman Avenue, South Black Avenue, and South Tracy Avenue between Main and Koch streets, but the density of residential development remained low, with only six to eight homes occupying a square block. Northside residential growth was limited to the two blocks immediately northeast of the commercial core, around the East Side School (later the site of Hawthorne School, **site 48**). Beginning in 1889, Sanborn maps also show early development related to the Northern Pacific Railroad, such as the Story Mill complex (**sites 39–42**) north of town and the beginning of a northeast neighborhood. Northern Pacific facilities appear on all of Bozeman bird's-eye maps but are not portrayed on Sanborn maps until 1904, two decades after Northern Pacific trains first steamed into Bozeman.

An 1898 bird's-eye map shows a maturing Bozeman: its hopes of becoming Montana's capital city had spurred rapid

*Only a few homes had been built near Cooper Park when promoters produced this 1898 bird's-eye view. Much of the land between the park (the rectangular block with center oval) and the Montana Agricultural College (lower right) remained undeveloped until the early decades of the twentieth century. Montana Hall and Taylor Hall (**sites 145 and 149**) are accurately depicted in their early campus settings.* PIONEER MUSEUM

development along Main Street. Residentially, the city had grown too, despite the Panic of 1893. Northeast of Main Street, residential development, especially along North Church and North Wallace avenues, suggests the relatively large number of workers employed by the nearby Northern Pacific rail yards, Julius Lehrkind's Bozeman Brewery at 803 North Wallace Avenue (**site 47**), and the Story Mill complex located north of the rail yards. Spur lines connected Nelson Story's mill with the Northern Pacific main line, and Bozeman's new streetcar track wound its way along streets and avenues between the young college campus and the Northern Pacific facilities. Southside development also slowly continued to grow, with homeowners drawn that direction by the college. Still, only a few homes stood as far south as Dickerson Street. In 1898, Bozeman remained a small town of just over three thousand residents.

Nevertheless, the forces that shaped Bozeman were firmly in place. After the turn of the century, the railroad and agricultural-processing facilities led to the growth of a working-class neighborhood northeast of Main Street while the college drew middle-class home builders to the south. Prosperity begat prosperity. In 1907, a Bozeman newspaper noted the disparity in residential development between the north and south sides: "The large proportion of improvements have been done on the south and southwest side of the city. Nothing has been done, at least nothing to speak of, on the north side. The consequence is property on the south side is vastly more valuable than that on the north side and many who formerly lived north of Main Street

*This circa 1890 image reveals the town's slow growth to the west and north of Main Street. This view looking southeast shows the Nelson Story Mansion (center), which stood on the grounds of what is today's Willson School at 404 West Main Street (**site 3**). The original Gallatin County Courthouse, the large building on the far left, was demolished in 1936.* PIONEER MUSEUM

have moved across the line." As the decades wore on, the north side developed a distinctly working-class character while the south side increasingly became home to the city's growing middle and upper-middle classes.

These general patterns, reflected on early Bozeman maps, do not do justice to the variety and nuances of Bozeman's development. Let us look, then, more closely at some of the buildings that line the streets of Bozeman's historic neighborhoods.

SELECTED MAIN STREET
HISTORIC DISTRICT SITES

1. Gallatin County Jail, 317 West Main Street, 1911
2. Gallatin County Courthouse, 311 West Main Street, 1936
3. Gallatin County High School and Willson School, 404 West Main Street, 1902 and 1936
4. Holy Rosary Church, 220 West Main Street, 1908
5. Baxter Hotel, 105 West Main Street, 1929
6. Benepe Building, 104–108 West Main Street, 1883
7. Bon Ton Bakery Building, 34–42 West Main Street, c. 1888, remodeled 1928
8. Ellen Theater, 17 West Main Street, 1919
9. Rialto Theater, 10 West Main Street, 1925
10. Gallatin State Bank Building, 2 West Main Street, 1908
11. National Bank of Gallatin Valley Building, 1 West Main Street, 1906
12. Avant-Courier Building, 1 East Main Street, 1879, remodeled 1881
13. Gem Theater, 18 East Main Street, 1908
14. Lamme Block, 23–29 East Main Street, 1883
15. Story Block, 33–39 East Main Street, 1901
16. Willson Building, 101 East Main Street, 1903
17. Cooper/Black Building, 118 East Main Street, 1872
18. Palace Saloon, 135 East Main Street, 1883
19. Fechter Hotel Building, 128–134 East Main Street, 1918
20. Harper Blacksmith Shop, 237 East Main Street, 1873
21. Spieth and Krug Brewery Building, 240–246 East Main Street, 1883
22. Electric Block, 316 East Main Street, 1901, remodeled 1945
23. Bozeman Hotel, 321 East Main Street, 1891
24. Hamill Apartment Building, 427 East Main Street, 1931
25. Northern Pacific Freight Depot, 611 East Main Street, c. 1908
26. Nash-Finch Building, 612 East Main Street, 1916
27. Female Boardinghouse, 234 East Mendenhall Street, 1891
28. Carnegie Library, 35 North Bozeman Avenue, 1904
29. National Guard Armory, 24 West Mendenhall Street, 1941
30. Nelson Story House, 322 West Mendenhall Street, c. 1869
62. Post Office Building, 32 South Tracy Avenue, 1915
64. Emerson School, 111 South Grand Avenue, 1919

BOZEMAN'S HISTORIC MAIN STREET

A STREETSCAPE THAT REFLECTS both a thriving past and an evolving present, Bozeman's historic Main Street is the heart of the city. Before its growth into a business district, Main Street was lined with houses between Willson (then Central) and Bozeman avenues. Nelson Story's first home, for example, was located downtown. This home, which may be Bozeman's oldest building, has been moved twice, first in 1890 from its location on the southeast corner of Main Street and Tracy Avenue to the nearby northeast corner of East Babcock Street and Tracy Avenue. In 1914, when construction of the brick Post Office Building (**site 62**) began at 32 South Tracy Avenue, the residence was moved again to its current home at 322 West Mendenhall Street (**site 30**).

Early Bozeman's false-front, wood-frame Main Street commercial buildings were commonly built as one-part commercial blocks. These simple, inexpensive buildings created a "downtown" business district by crowding against one another along Main Street. As one historian declared, they "represented a claim staked on urban ground" that would eventually support larger, more substantial business blocks.

Commercial buildings along Main Street reflect on the city's history from 1872 to the present. Most numerous are buildings from the eras of active growth: the 1880s, when Bozeman incorporated and the Northern Pacific Railroad arrived, and 1900 to 1925, when Bozeman solidified its role as the Gallatin Valley's commercial center.

Nearly a quarter of the buildings within the Main Street Historic District date from the last two decades of the nineteenth century, and most of these buildings are located along the eastern portion of Main Street. Fortunately, two buildings remain from the 1870s: Walter Cooper and Colonel Leander Black's 1872 two-story brick armory at 118 East Main Street (**site 17**) and the small brick building across the street from the armory at 237 East Main Street (**site 20**), built by blacksmith Frank Harper for his shop in 1873.

Both Black and Cooper came to Bozeman in the late 1860s, Black after working as a miner in the Pikes Peak gold rush and Cooper after years of fur trading, mining, and freighting. The men shared a vision of Bozeman as a commercial hub for expanding local and regional markets. Construction of their imposing brick building began in summer 1872, and by December, the completed structure dwarfed the wood-frame buildings that surrounded it. Cooper's armory supplied weapons to trappers and buffalo hunters, and during the 1870s, Bozeman became a primary shipping point for furs and hides. Black's profitable mercantile shared the ground floor with Cooper's armory. Signaling the wealth of its frontier merchant owners, the Cooper/Black Building was a milestone for early Bozeman, and its sheer size surely made an impression on those

*The two-story Cooper/Black Building at 118 East Main Street (**site 17**), pictured here shortly after its 1872 construction, housed five businesses: Walter Cooper's armory, Leander Black's general store, a drug store, a meat market, and a second mercantile. Despite alterations, the building remains one of the most historically significant buildings in Bozeman.* MOR

passing through town. Just two-thirds of the 1872 building, or seven of the original eleven bays, remains today.

Brick buildings like the Cooper/Black Building had special meaning to Montana's settlers. The durable material reminded newcomers of their former lives in the East. Brick also signaled permanence. In a region where a town's future depended on the health of nearby mineral veins, brick buildings were emblems of stability. It wasn't long before Bozeman had its

*A brick shortage in 1883 slowed construction of Spieth and Krug's Brewery at 240–246 East Main Street (**site 21**) so much that the brewers settled for different-colored bricks on the first and second floors—a pragmatic decision still evident today.* AUTHOR

own locally produced supply of brick, and by the mid-1870s, demand for brick had increased enough to keep two local brickworks running at full capacity.

Other pre-railroad buildings include the longtime home of the *Avant-Courier* at 1 East Main Street (**site 12**). Built in 1879, remodeled in 1881, and recently restored, the two-story brick commercial block housed the popular local newspaper founded by Bozeman pioneer William W. Alderson in 1871. Like most frontier newspapers, the *Avant-Courier* filled its columns with signs of Bozeman's progress and paeans to its prosperous future.

Another successful Bozeman entrepreneur, Frank Benepe, also left his mark on Main Street in the form of his commercial building at 104–108 West Main Street (**site 6**). Michael Leeson's *History of Montana* tells us that Benepe "bought and sold more grain than any man in the Gallatin Valley." The owner of a large valley farm, Benepe immediately took advantage of the arrival of the railroad, building grain elevators near the new Northern Pacific facilities. He also took advantage of family connections and began construction of his commercial block in 1883 on land he purchased from his brother-in-law, Nelson Story.

*While the ground floor of Frank Benepe's 1883 commercial building at 104–108 West Main Street (*site 6*) has been altered, the building still reflects the reason behind its construction. On the building's west side, a faint ghost sign not visible in this modern photograph reads, "F. L. Benepe Agricultural Implements."* AUTHOR

Early in 1883, with the arrival of the Northern Pacific literally just over the eastern horizon, the *Avant-Courier* stated with confidence: "The prospect is now that there will be double the building of business blocks and residences ever before known in the history of the city of Bozeman." Three buildings constructed in 1883 to greet Northern Pacific travelers still stand: the Gothic Revival–style Palace Saloon at 135 East Main Street (**site 18**), the Commercial Italianate–style Lamme Block at 23–29 East Main Street (**site 14**), and Jacob Spieth and Charles Krug's Italianate Brewery at 240–246 East Main Street (**site 21**).

Noted local architect Byron Vreeland and partner Herman Kemna designed the Palace Saloon, described in its heyday as "the finest saloon west of Chicago." Though smaller than the Palace Saloon, the Lamme Block was equally lavish. Constructed as the headquarters of merchant and physician Achilles Lamme, the building is the finest example of the Italianate style in downtown Bozeman.

Spieth and Krug were German immigrants who originally passed through Bozeman in the early 1860s on their way to the goldfields. They returned to Bozeman in 1867 and opened a brewery in a wooden building near Bozeman Creek, the source of the water they used for their beer. When their wood-frame brewery burned, they rebuilt in brick. The brewery became a gathering place for Fort Ellis officers and Bozeman's small upper class.

Many of the buildings constructed during this decade and subsequent ones are two-part commercial blocks, the most common form for nineteenth- and early-twentieth-century downtown buildings. These multi-story buildings visually dis-

*Dr. Achilles Lamme's 1883 business block at 23–29 East Main Street (**site 14**) epitomizes the changes the arrival of the Northern Pacific brought to Main Street. Confident of the community's future, investors like Lamme increasingly replaced early false-front buildings with stylish brick business blocks. Lamme's building features an elegantly bracketed cornice, decorative window hood moldings, and stone corner quoins that reflect the Commercial Italianate style.* PIONEER MUSEUM

tinguish the first floor from the upper stories (hence the "two parts"). Their Main Street level spaces were public zones used for retail shops or banks. Their upper floors accommodated more private uses—offices, meeting halls for private lodges, and, eventually, apartments. The Avant-Courier Building at 1 East Main Street (**site 12**) was typical. In 1883, Kleinschmidt and Bro.'s grocery store and the *Courier*'s business and editorial rooms occupied the first floor. The second floor provided office space for real estate brokers, doctors, and attorneys.

With a design that combined Italianate and Second Empire influences, the Nelson Story Mansion on West Main Street, shown here in an early 1890s photograph, overshadowed Bozeman's other early buildings. Note the grazing horse in the Storys' front yard. MHS

Early Main Street also featured residences, including Nelson Story's impressive Second Empire–style mansion built in 1888 and designed to outdo lavish residences in the more established towns of Helena and Butte. Local newspapers provided their readers with running commentary on the home's construction—it was the pride of Bozeman. One 1886 article described how Story and architect Byron Vreeland traveled east to purchase plumbing and hardware supplies, noting that

when the home was "completed [it would] be the most imposing and costly residence in the territory. Story never does
anything by halves." Five decades later, high maintenance costs
led the Story family to sell the palatial residence to allow for the
expansion of the Gallatin County High School at 404 West Main
Street, today's Willson School (**site 3**). The marble columns,
which once flanked the front entrance to Story's mansion, are
today located at the Story family plot at Sunset Hills Cemetery,
a reminder of Story's seminal role in building Bozeman.

Though Main Street was still choked with dust in the
summer and with mud in the winter (concrete sidewalks were
not installed until 1907), the 1890s commenced with a fevered
but ultimately unsuccessful attempt to become the state capital.
Urbanization continued with the construction of several
architectural gems dedicated to cultivating an urbane image
for the fledgling community. Calls for a modern hotel, sounded
since the early 1880s, were answered in 1891 with the
completion of the Bozeman Hotel at 321 East Main Street (**site
23**). Along with the opulent Bozeman City Hall and Opera
House (built in 1890 and demolished in 1966), the new hotel
reflected Bozeman's determined bid to become the capital of
the newly formed state of Montana.

That bid, of course, never materialized, and things looked
bleak for Bozeman as the Panic of 1893, a nationwide
depression that dwarfed the economic problems of the 1870s,
stifled development. Amidst this economic tumult, however,
came the Montana Agricultural College. The arrival of the
college had a long-term effect on the economy and patterns of
real estate development. The college, which became the largest

*The most prominent of architect George Hancock's local designs, the Bozeman Hotel at 321 East Main Street (left, **site 23**), across from the Tilton Building, was a centerpiece of the campaign to urbanize and refine the city. Financed by the Bozeman Improvement Association for $120,000, the hotel was completed in March 1891. Steam heat, electricity, and 136 guest rooms attracted a "flattering patronage" to the state-of-the-art accommodations. The Tilton Building, a mercantile, was demolished in the 1960s to build today's City Hall. MOR*

employer in town, has arguably been of greater sustained benefit to Bozeman than the capital would have been. As Lester Willson sagely proclaimed in the *Avant-Courier*: "[I]n the long run . . . the Agricultural College will be preferable to the capital. The people here do not as yet fully appreciate the information of the new institution."

Among those taking advantage of the possibilities created by the college was Nelson Story, who, in 1901, built the Story Block, one of the largest commercial blocks in the district at that time, at 33–39 East Main Street (**site 15**). Story constructed the building solely as an investment. He rented portions of his multi-unit building to other business owners, which was a departure from previous Main Street buildings that owners occupied with enterprises of their own.

Across North Black Avenue, Civil War Union general Lester Willson built the 1903 L. S. Willson and Co. Mercantile at 101 East Main Street (**site 16**). Quartermaster general for Montana Territory from 1883 to 1886, Willson had connections about which other local capitalists could only dream. His two-story brick business block still stands at the northeast corner of Main Street and Black Avenue.

Following the turn of the century, Bozeman's Main Street projected a more urbane image, and locals could travel its length on electrified trolleys or window shop on new sidewalks. A reminder of Bozeman's early transportation system can be found at today's Eagles Lodge at 316 East Main Street (**site 22**). Known historically as the Electric Block, the building served as the headquarters of the Gallatin Light, Power, and Railway Company.

*The presence of the Holy Rosary Church at 220 West Main Street (**site 4**, left) and other downtown churches suggests that Bozeman's downtown served as the social and spiritual center of the city as well as its commercial hub. This postcard dates from the 1910s.* MHS

In 1908, the Holy Rosary Church at 220 West Main Street (**site 4**) added a different architectural style to Main Street. The Gothic Revival–style church emphasizes verticality with its sharply pointed spire (a second spire has been removed), a prominent rose window, paired lancet windows, and buttresses. The building recalled the Catholic Church's power in the Middle Ages and, like those who worshipped within it, reached upwards toward the heavens.

Downtown schools are an important exception to the high building density of Main Street. Like civic buildings, schools

were surrounded by open space; physically setting such structures apart emphasized their social importance just as much
as did the buildings' mass and architectural flair. The 1902
Gallatin County High School at 404 West Main Street (**site 3**) is
a good example of the way open space was used to distinguish
civic buildings from their commercial neighbors.

At the turn of the century, as now, national economic trends
had a tremendous effect on the composition of Main Street

*The construction of
the National Bank of
Gallatin Valley
Building at 1 West
Main Street (**site 11**)
followed closely on the
heels of the Carnegie
Library at 35 North
Bozeman Avenue (**site
28**) and imitated its
classical sensibilities.
The bank's concrete
block construction,
seen here in a modern
photograph, is unique
along Main Street.*
Author

businesses. Farmers took out loans to invest in the technology offered by the State Agricultural Experiment Station, and new downtown banks prospered. The National Bank of Gallatin Valley Building at 1 West Main Street (**site 11**), built in 1906, retains its most prominent architectural detailing in the immense Doric columns that flank the entrance to the building. The building's stately Classical Revival style conveys a sense of security and stability—an irony since the bank closed as a result of the economic depression during the 1920s. The 1908 Gallatin State Bank Building at 2 West Main Street (**site 10**) is located directly across from its counterpart. Faithfully restored in 1992, the Classical Revival–style building features a recessed corner entrance (the only entry of its type on Main Street) flanked by Roman columns and topped with the original "GSB" molded sign.

In 1919, Woolworth's department store moved into the first floor of the brick and terra cotta Fechter Hotel Building at 128–134 East Main Street (**site 19**), marking a new development in the evolution of downtown—the entry of nationwide chain stores into Bozeman. Fred Willson designed the ornate building, which was completed in 1918. The two upper floors maintain Willson's fanciful detailing, including terra cotta gargoyles—a detail perhaps gleaned from his study in Europe. While much of the street-level façade has been altered, the decorative leaded-glass panels remain. New construction techniques and materials made these large windows possible: steel frames transferred the building weight around the window openings.

A very different type of new technology made its mark on Bozeman's Main Street when the Ellen Theater at 17 West Main

*Terra cotta made possible the wonderful Beaux Arts–style detail on the Fechter Hotel Building at 128–134 East Main (**site 19**). Imported from out-of-state manufacturers, the lightweight and easily produced material brought big-city glamour to growing Montana towns.* AUTHOR

Street (**site 8**) opened its doors in 1919. The Gem Theater at 18 East Main Street (**site 13**) had begun showing motion pictures in 1918 in an existing building, but the opulent Ellen, designed by Fred Willson and financed by members of the Story family, was the first Bozeman theater designed specifically with movies in mind. Then, in 1925, the Rialto Theater opened at 10 West Main (**site 9**). In 1934, the Rialto temporarily moved into the former post office while Fred Willson directed an extensive interior remodel. After a 1967 fire destroyed the original Rialto marquee and storefront, owners added the present façade.

*A long line stretches past the Chambers-Fisher Building (center) and the National Bank of Gallatin Valley Building (**site 11**, right), testifying to the popularity of the Ellen Theater (**site 8**), named by the Story sons for their mother. The theater hosted films, live theater, and musical performances. A banquet hall upstairs provided the Storys space for private parties.* PIONEER MUSEUM

The Ellen Theater and the Story Block at 33–39 East Main Street (**site 15**) are reminders of the Story family's impact on Bozeman's built environment. The Ellen also reflects architect Fred Willson's lasting legacy. But more than in any single design, Willson's influence on Bozeman's Main Street architecture is manifest in the sheer number of buildings he worked on. In the late 1920s, he overhauled Eugene Graf's Bon Ton Bakery Building at 34–42 West Main Street (**site 7**), creating the colorful Mission Revival–façade that remains today. He then capped the 1920s by designing Main Street's grandest edifice, the Baxter Hotel at 105 West Main Street (**site 5**). When the hotel opened in 1929, the *Bozeman Daily Chronicle* hailed it as "the beginning of a new order of things in Bozeman."

As in so much else, the Great Depression serves as a dividing line in architecture. The Streamlined Moderne style came to the fore as architects looked for an inexpensive but distinctive building style. By mimicking modern transportation's

*The 1929 seven-story Baxter Hotel at 105 West Main Street (**site 5**) is a showcase of Fred Willson's skill as an architect. In his design, Willson combined classical elements, such as the paired columns between the top floor windows and the medallions above those windows, with elements from the emerging Moderne movement, including the simple cornice and stepped parapet. Willson even included Art Nouveau porticos on the Main Street and North Willson Avenue entrances. The hotel testifies to the faith Bozemanites had in their city's future as a tourist destination. When construction funding fell short, residents' stock purchases filled the gap. MOR*

*Designed in the Moderne style popular during the New Deal era, Gallatin County's 1936 courthouse at 311 West Main Street (**site 2**) was one of several federally financed projects that brought jobs and civic improvements to Bozeman during the Great Depression.* MOR

aerodynamic lines and smooth surfaces, the style celebrates the era's technological advances, symbols of hope during an otherwise bleak period.

Fred Willson embraced the Moderne movement, first with the 1931 design of the Hamill Apartment Building at 427 East Main Street (**site 24**). New Deal funding made Willson's larger Moderne designs possible. The WPA underwrote both the construction of the Willson-designed Gallatin County Courthouse at 311 West Main Street (**site 2**) and the demolition of the old county courthouse in 1936. Willson continued his Moderne-influenced work across Main Street in a WPA-funded addition to the original 1902 Gallatin County High School at 404 West Main Street, today's Willson School (**site 3**). New schools and government centers like these sought to strengthen ordinary Americans' faith in their government and to counter the Great Depression's heavy toll on public morale.

With the exception of the 1941 Moderne-style National Guard Armory at 24 West Mendenhall Street (**site 29**), designed by Fred Willson, almost all construction stopped during World War II as the country diverted manpower and material to the war effort. Though postwar demolition cost Bozeman the City Hall and Opera House, little new construction occurred within Bozeman's historic core after the war, a fortunate turn of events that has helped preserve much of downtown Bozeman's historic feel. More recently, a growing appreciation for historic architecture has brought businesses and customers back downtown as developers restore buildings that sat empty for decades, adapting them for contemporary use.

*The 1936 addition of a middle school to the Gallatin County High School at 404 West Main Street (**site 3**) resulted in the demolition of the Nelson Story Mansion (above), one of Bozeman's most prominent early landmarks. In 1956, the school was named the Willson School in honor of the building's famed architect.* PIONEER MUSEUM

NORTH SIDE HISTORIC NEIGHBORHOODS

UNLIKE IN A TRADITIONAL RAILROAD TOWN, where the rails separated the respectable business district from the bars and brothels on the "wrong side of the tracks," Bozeman's social geography was less well defined. In the 1870s through the turn of the century, the red-light district flourished just north of Main Street and west of North Rouse Avenue. One building remains on East Mendenhall Street to represent the early "female boardinghouses," the nineteenth century's euphemism for brothels. The size and solidity of the 1891 two-story brick building at 234 East Mendenhall Street (**site 27**) suggests just how profitable and accepted prostitution was in the late nineteenth century.

Eager to extend Main Street's growing respectability northward, Progressive Era reformers sited the town's new library at 35 North Bozeman Avenue (**site 28**) across from the red-light district in 1904. Moral crusaders firmly believed that the Classical Revival–style Carnegie Library, designed by Montana architect C. S. Haire, would have an elevating effect on the district. In this, they echoed national City Beautiful advocates, who believed that improving "the landscape [would] complement the burgeoning reforms in other areas of society."

NORTH SIDE HISTORIC
DISTRICTS AND SELECTED SITES

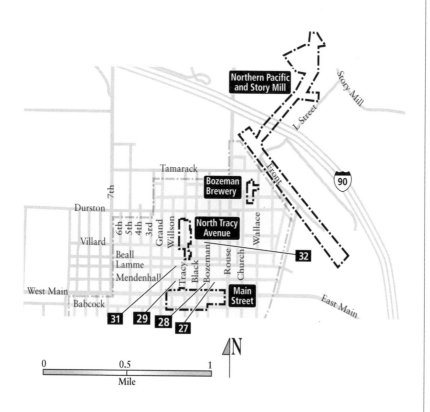

27. Female Boardinghouse, 234 East Mendenhall Street, 1891
28. Carnegie Library, 35 North Bozeman Avenue, 1904
29. National Guard Armory, 24 West Mendenhall Street, 1941
31. Bozeman Deaconess Hospital, 15 West Lamme Street, 1919,
    remodeled 1944 and 1971
32. Beall Park Community Center, 409 North Bozeman Avenue, 1927

*Steel magnate Andrew Carnegie funded nearly two thousand libraries in the United States, including seventeen in Montana. Many, like Bozeman's Carnegie Library at 35 North Bozeman Avenue (**site 28**), shown here in an early-twentieth-century photograph, had symmetrical "temple front" façades—an appropriate choice for these "temples of learning." MHS*

However, this desired effect was still years away. Sanborn maps from 1904 and 1912 demonstrate the continuing presence of female boardinghouses in the quarter, referred to as "Bozeman Alley" in the city directory. In 1917, the state attorney general called for the shutdown of red-light districts across the state, and police crackdowns effectively closed the brothels of Bozeman Alley.

Other buildings north of Main have their own stories to tell. The imposing Bozeman Deaconess Hospital at 15 West Lamme Street (**site 31**), for example, was not the first hospital in Bozeman, but it was the first building built expressly for that purpose. Designed by Fred Willson in 1918, the hospital was completed the following year. The Classical Revival–style building represented a milestone in Bozeman's coming of age. In 1944, the federal government funded the west wing addition to accommodate a new nursing program created to meet the growing demand for nurses due to World War II. An east wing, adjacent to the main entrance, was built in 1971, unfortunately compromising much of this significant building's architectural integrity.

Another notable landmark on the north side is the Beall Park Community Center at 409 North Bozeman Avenue (**site 32**) just a few blocks from the hospital. The park itself is located on the original homestead of town co-founder William J. Beall, and the land was purchased from his widow, Rosa.

*An architecturally impressive two-story, four-column marble portico surrounds the marble entrance of the historic Bozeman Deaconess Hospital at 15 West Lamme Street (**site 31**). Prior to the construction of a 1971 addition, this Fred Willson–designed building was the finest local example of the Classical Revival style.* AUTHOR

*The Craftsman-style features of the 1927 Beall Park Community Center at 409 North Bozeman Avenue (**site 32**), seen here in a 2006 photograph, include its cobblestone and fieldstone exterior, overhanging eaves, exposed rafter tails, and decorative brackets.* AUTHOR

Funding for the center was donated by local philanthropist Ella T. Martin, who sought to found "a community center where young and old of Gallatin Valley may gather and enjoy themselves and indulge themselves in wholesome recreation," a sentiment typical of the Progressive Era. Designed in 1927 by architect and engineer W. R. Plew, who helped launch the first architectural courses at the college, it is one of the finest examples of Craftsman-style architecture found in the city.

Northern Pacific and Story Mill Historic District

NORTHEAST OF DOWNTOWN, near the railroad tracks, is the Northern Pacific and Story Mill Historic District, Bozeman's historic industrial core. John V. Bogert, Bozeman's first mayor

*The Northern Pacific Passsenger Depot at 820 Front Street (**site 36**) buzzes with activity in this World War II–era image. In 1924, the Northern Pacific abandoned the standardized plans it generally relied upon for company buildings and retained architect Fred Willson to renovate the passenger depot. Today, the building sits deserted and vandalized on Front Street. MHS*

after the community incorporated, platted the Northern Pacific Addition in 1883. Shortly thereafter, the Northern Pacific Railroad extended its transcontinental line through Bozeman. The Northern Pacific railroad facilities, which anchor the southern portion of the district, grew at a rate that matched Bozeman's burgeoning farm economy.

The railroad operated from a wood-frame depot for nearly ten years, despite local newspaper criticism that described the depot as "a standing disgrace, both to the city and railroad company." The city finally received the new brick passenger depot at 820 Front Street (**site 36**) in 1892 as part of an improvement campaign undertaken in an effort to secure the state capital for Bozeman. In 1924, Fred Willson designed an addition for the depot's west elevation, stylistically updating the Victorian Era building with Craftsman- and Prairie-style features. Today, the passenger depot sits neglected and unused—evidence of the transition from a railroad- to auto-centered economy.

The Northern Pacific demolished many of its other facilities following World War II, but some of the warehouses built along the tracks still stand, including the Northern Pacific's own freight house at 506–526 Front Street (**site 33**). Though modified, the building is an example of the standardized design common to railroad structures across the country. Other railroad-related warehouses include the General Warehouse Building at 704 Front Street (**site 34**) and the Lindsay Fruit Company Warehouse at 720 Front Street (**site 35**), both constructed between 1904 and 1908. These utilitarian masonry buildings—now adapted to modern uses—were significant components of the railroad economy central to Bozeman's

SELECTED NORTHERN PACIFIC AND STORY MILL HISTORIC DISTRICT SITES

33. Northern Pacific Freight Building, 506–526 Front Street, 1883, 1909
34. General Warehouse Building, 704 Front Street, pre-1908
35. Lindsay Fruit Company Warehouse, 720 Front Street, pre-1908
36. Northern Pacific Passenger Depot, 820 Front Street, 1892, 1924
37. Story Mill spillway and canal remains, c. 1882
38. Bozeman Livestock Auction Yards, c. 1930s
39. Metal grain bins, 1943
40. Concrete grain bins, c. 1920s
41. Mill complex: Story Mill Building, c. 1903, grain elevator, c. 1903, and attached brick warehouses, c. 1883 and 1912
42. Head miller's house, c. 1892

SELECTED NORTHERN PACIFIC AND STORY MILL HISTORIC DISTRICT SITES

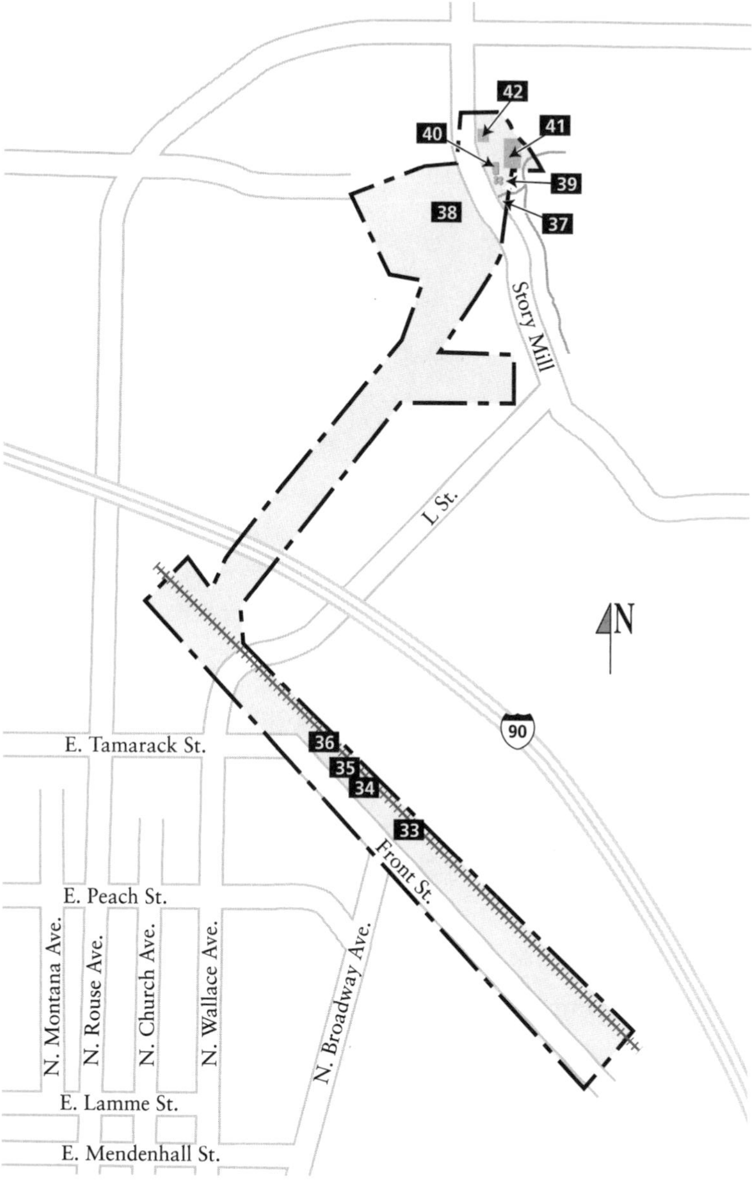

42

40

41

39

38

37

Story Mill

L St.

N

90

E. Tamarack St.

36

35

34

33

E. Peach St.

Front St.

N. Montana Ave.

N. Rouse Ave.

N. Church Ave.

N. Wallace Ave.

N. Broadway Ave.

E. Lamme St.

E. Mendenhall St.

Direct access to the Northern Pacific main line gave Nelson Story a tremendous business advantage. In just two years after the arrival of the railroad, Story built what was reputed to be the largest mill complex in Montana (sites 39–42). The photograph above was taken before the devastating 1901 fire. MHS

growth in the first half of the twentieth century.

The district also contains Nelson Story's flour mill, which predated the arrival of the railroad. Story's influence was such, however, that by offering the Northern Pacific a right-of-way across his land, he persuaded the railroad to build a spur line to connect his mill with the main line. When the tracks through town were completed, Story's business was the only one to have its own line.

The spur line turned out to have one surprising disadvantage. In 1901, sparks from a railcar started a fire that destroyed much of Story's original mill complex. Nevertheless, important elements of the original mill stand today. An engineering marvel in its day, the canal system (**site 37**) powered the mill into the 1950s; it still weaves along the Story Hills. The head miller's brick Queen Anne–style residence (**site 42**) also survived the fire, as did the oldest building at the mill, an 1883 brick warehouse attached to the eastern portion of the five-story, brick mill building completed shortly after the fire. The massive six-and-one-half-story grain elevator, with its fading "It's the Wheat Flour" ghost sign, was completed circa 1903 and is located immediately west of the original masonry mill building (**site 41**).

The rebuilt brick mill commenced operation in 1904. With these improved facilities, the Story Mill further captured the market for central Montana wheat milling and storage. The

Hat in hand, a mill worker tries to answer an irate Nelson Story's questions following the 1901 fire that devastated Story's mill. MOR

prosperity of the millworks continued into the twentieth century under the direction of Thomas B. "T. B." Story, who took over the family business after his father's retirement.

A second transcontinental railroad, the Chicago, Milwaukee & St. Paul, reached Bozeman in 1911 and built its own spur to the mill complex in 1914. In anticipation, T. B. Story ordered a new round of improvements to the mill, including the construction of a large new brick warehouse designed by Fred Willson, attached to the northern portion of the brick mill complex.

In 1918, Story sold the mill to the Montana Flour Mills Company. Montana Mills added six large concrete grain bins (**site 40**) in the 1920s, and in 1943, the company constructed four large steel grain bins (**site 39**)—perhaps the most visually dominating structure in the district today.

Although the Story family sold their interest in the mill in 1918, they retained ownership of nearby land. There, T. B.'s son, Malcolm Story, established the Bozeman Livestock Auction Yards (**site 38**) in the 1930s.

Bozeman Brewery Historic District

JUST SOUTH OF THE NORTHERN PACIFIC and Story Mill Historic District is another reminder of Bozeman's industrial past: the Bozeman Brewery Historic District. German immigrant Julius Lehrkind honed his brewing skills at a Philadelphia brewery before he and his brother, Fred, opened their own brewery in Davenport, Iowa, in 1868. After twenty-six years in Iowa, the already prosperous Julius Lehrkind came to Bozeman in 1894, bringing a large family—five children, as well as the four children of his deceased brother and sister-in-law—and a crew

*In its heyday, Julius Lehrkind's immense Bozeman Brewery at 803 North Wallace Avenue (**site 47**, pictured here circa 1905) produced forty thousand barrels of beer annually and had a full twelve thousand square feet of refrigeration space.* COB

of trusted and skilled brewery workers with him. He purchased the popular Main Street brewery of Spieth and Krug but relocated the operation to his new facilities on the sparsely populated northern edge of town. Lehrkind was as shrewd a businessman as he was a skilled brewmaster—building his new brewery near the Northern Pacific rail yards guaranteed him quick access to commercial transportation and supply. He also operated the Red Lodge Brewery in Red Lodge.

The 1895 Bozeman Brewery at 803 North Wallace Avenue (**site 47**) was Bozeman's largest building until the university completed its new field house in 1957. In 1898, Lehrkind

SELECTED BOZEMAN BREWERY HISTORIC DISTRICT AND NORTHEAST NEIGHBORHOOD SITES

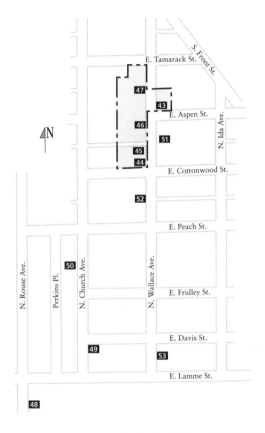

43. Lehrkind Bottling Plant, 802 North Wallace Avenue, 1925
44. Edwin Lehrkind House, 701 North Wallace Avenue, 1912
45. Henry Lehrkind House, 707 North Wallace Avenue, 1908
46. Lehrkind Mansion, 719 North Wallace Avenue, 1898
47. Bozeman Brewery, 803 North Wallace Avenue, 1895
48. Hawthorne School, 114 North Rouse Avenue, 1939
49. Busch House, 224 North Church Avenue, c. 1895
50. Hill House, 415 North Church Avenue, c. 1893
51. MISCO Grain Elevator, 700 North Wallace Avenue, 1933
52. Bon Ton Mills, 611 North Wallace Avenue, 1932
53. Peterson House, 216 North Wallace Avenue, c. 1895

*The impeccably maintained Lehrkind Mansion at 719 North Wallace Avenue (**site 46**) expresses many of the finer elements of the Queen Anne style in its six-sided corner turret, elaborate porch, and sharply gabled roof with decorative roofline.* AUTHOR

completed construction of a two-and-one-half-story Queen Anne–style residence at 719 North Wallace Avenue (**site 46**) next to the brewery. Two of Lehrkind's closest relatives soon built homes south of his mansion. His nephew, Henry, constructed a Colonial Revival–style house at 707 North Wallace Avenue (**site 45**) in 1908, and four years later Lehrkind's son, Edwin, built his own home, a bungalow, at 701 North Wallace Avenue (**site 44**). The business was very much a family affair, as this cluster of Lerhkind family residences near the brewery attests.

Prohibition hit the Lehkind family hard, and the brewery suffered, especially following Julius's death in 1922. Large portions of the brewery and a nearby maltinghouse were demolished. Nevertheless, the family persevered, entering the soft-drink business and constructing a one-story brick bottling plant at 802 North Wallace Avenue (**site 43**) in 1925. In fact, Lehrkind descendants still bottle and distribute soft drinks.

Northeast Neighborhood

PART OF THE LEHRKIND MANSION'S DISTINCTIVE QUALITY is its location near the railroad tracks, amidst the northeast neighborhood, one of Bozeman's earliest working-class neighborhoods. The neighborhood developed as a direct result of the railroad. With the trains came people—Bozeman ballooned from a population of approximately nine hundred in 1880 to an estimated three thousand in 1883—and these people needed somewhere to live. Predictably, the laboring men who worked for the railroad settled near the rail yards.

The 1892 city directory lists ninety-seven men (the directory counted only men and widowed women) living in the neighborhood, generally along North Church and North Wallace Avenues between Mendenhall and Peach streets. Over half of them worked for the Northern Pacific. The other half reflected the diversity of professions and nationalities for which the northeast neighborhood became known. There were Swiss dressmakers, German cigar makers, French masons, and Missouri miners. Ethnically, the railroad workers

Bozeman residents dubbed William Babcock's regal residence the "Castle." This early North Church Avenue home was destroyed in an 1880s fire and its remains were subsequently demolished. PIONEER MUSEUM

were equally diverse, hailing as they did from Canada, Sweden, Scotland, and elsewhere.

Railroad workers lived in a variety of circumstances, with many boarding together in homes all over the neighborhood. Emory G. B. Hill resided at 415 North Church Avenue (**site 50**) for decades after arriving in Bozeman in 1890 to work as an engineer. In 1925, Hill was elected to the Bozeman City Commission and by 1929 assumed the post of mayor, the first to hail from the northeast neighborhood. Hill's neighbor and fellow railroad man Apollo Busch also resided on North Church Street for years. Busch constructed his fine brick-veneered, one-and-one-half-story,

*One result of the industrialization in the last decades of the nineteenth century was that building materials could be inexpensively manufactured and sent by rail to remote corners of the country, putting decorative architectural flourishes within reach of ordinary Americans for the first time. James Peterson, a laborer and teamster for the Kenyon-Noble Lumber Company, incorporated prefabricated spindlework and trim into his gable-front-and-wing home at 216 North Wallace Avenue (**site 53**) built circa 1895.* AUTHOR

Queen Anne–style cottage at 224 North Church Avenue (**site 49**) circa 1895. Initially a foreman for the Northern Pacific, he served several terms on the city commission and was eventually hired as superintendent of the Gallatin Valley Electric Railway, which, co-incidentally, maintained service past his North Church home.

Reminders of Bozeman's agricultural past stand alongside the historic homes of the northeast neighborhood. Among them are the remains of Eugene Graf's Bon Ton Mills at 611 North Wallace Avenue (**site 52**). Designed by Fred Willson and constructed in 1932 in the early years of the Great Depression, the mills processed the flour Graf used at his bakery. Like the Bon Ton Mills, the MISCO Grain Elevator at 700 North Wallace Avenue (**site 51**) provides a reminder of agriculture's role in building the town. Built in 1933 by the Missoula Mercantile Company, the five-story grain elevator is the finest remaining

*In 2002, the City of Bozeman honored the owners of the MISCO Grain Elevator at 700 North Wallace Avenue (**site 51**) with an "Excellence in Historic Preservation" award for their successful efforts to revitalize and reuse this important part of Bozeman's agricultural heritage.* AUTHOR

example of agricultural architecture in the city. In recent years, it was the subject of a sensitive rehabilitation that adapted the building to new uses while maintaining its historic integrity.

Today's residents highly value the northeast neighborhood's mixed industrial, agricultural, and residential features. In 2004, residents were instrumental in helping to form the Northeast Historic Mixed Use District, the community group created to help safeguard the integrity of the neighborhood. The group's literature notes that the "unique qualities and nature of the area are not found elsewhere in Bozeman" and asserts that the neighborhood "should be preserved as a place offering additional opportunities for creative integration of land uses."

North Tracy Avenue Historic District

IN 1885 AND 1891, BOZEMAN PIONEER WILLIAM BEALL platted the two additions that make up this historic district. Beall likely hoped to capitalize on the growth sparked by the arrival of the railroad, and this neighborhood, too, became home to members of the working class.

The neighborhood's earliest residences are good examples of vernacular-style architecture—houses based on traditional forms and built without an architect's expertise. African American carpenter George Harrison constructed his home, a brick I-House dwelling at 322 North Tracy Avenue (site 55) circa 1890. Today, it is one of few remaining examples of this I-House style in Bozeman. Harrison was not the only carpenter to settle in the neighborhood. Around the same time, carpenter and German immigrant William Toeppler built his simple wood-frame home (site 57) two blocks away at 506 North Tracy

Avenue. They are the earliest residences in the neighborhood.

Beall's 1892 advertisements promised that "the convenience to business centre, water mains, electric lights, etc., adds greatly to the value of this Addition." Nevertheless, the area remained less fashionable than neighborhoods to the south. Apart from the Harrison and Toeppler homes, little construction occurred until the late 1890s, when Bozeman began recovering from the Panic of 1893. Even then, the houses were modest. Built by local carpenters or the residents themselves, they generally lacked the "high style" character common to Bozeman's more elegant neighborhoods. One exception is valley rancher Edward

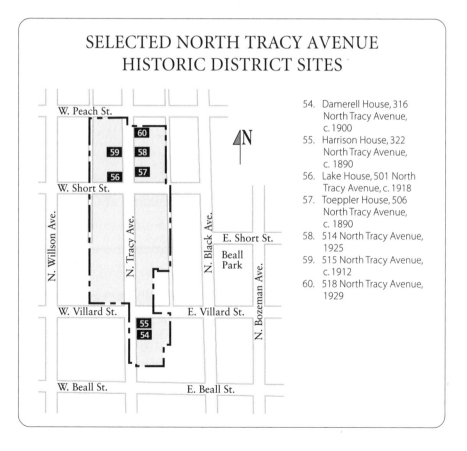

SELECTED NORTH TRACY AVENUE HISTORIC DISTRICT SITES

54. Damerell House, 316 North Tracy Avenue, c. 1900
55. Harrison House, 322 North Tracy Avenue, c. 1890
56. Lake House, 501 North Tracy Avenue, c. 1918
57. Toeppler House, 506 North Tracy Avenue, c. 1890
58. 514 North Tracy Avenue, 1925
59. 515 North Tracy Avenue, c. 1912
60. 518 North Tracy Avenue, 1929

*Likely constructed circa 1912, this wood-frame residence at 515 North Tracy Avenue (**site 59**) is a fine example of the type of modest homes common to north side working-class neighborhoods.* AUTHOR

Damerell's large, Colonial Revival–influenced home at 316 North Tracy Avenue (**site 54**), constructed circa 1900. More common to the neighborhood are modest Craftsman-style bungalows—a simplified version of the fashionable Craftsman style as promoted through architectural pattern books.

Pattern books gave builders the information they needed to construct stylish homes without the expense of hiring an architect—and their influence can be seen in the Craftsman-style exposed rafter tails, front dormers or centered gable-end windows, and prominent front porches that adorn many North Tracy bungalows. Good examples include the circa 1918 home constructed for painter August Lake at 501 North Tracy Avenue (**site 56**) and the 1925 and 1929 bungalows at 514 and

518 North Tracy Avenue (**sites 58 and 60**), built for resale by Lou Sievert, a name synonymous with bungalow residential construction all over Bozeman.

At one time, much of Bozeman's north side looked as North Tracy Avenue does now. The historic district is noteworthy, however, because it is one of the few north side neighborhoods to retain its architectural integrity. Today, its modest vernacular and pattern-book residences, built by and for area craftsmen, continue to recall the neighborhood's early-twentieth-century development and its working-class roots.

SOUTH SIDE HISTORIC NEIGHBORHOODS

THE NEIGHBORHOODS THAT MAKE UP BOZEMAN'S south side include some of the finest residential architecture found in Montana. But modest houses also line these streets, and they are as much a legacy of Bozeman's historical development as

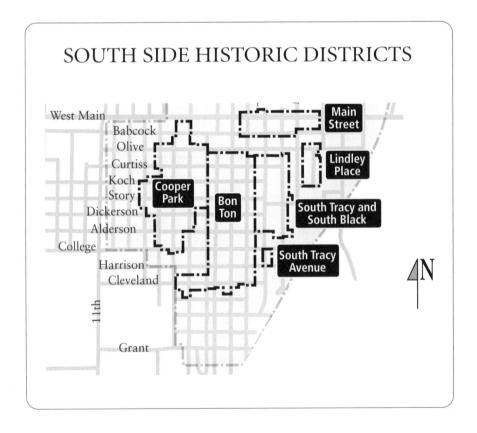

SOUTH SIDE HISTORIC DISTRICTS

West Main
Babcock
Olive
Curtiss
Koch
Story
Dickerson
Alderson
College
Harrison
Cleveland
11th
Grant

Cooper Park

Bon Ton

Main Street

Lindley Place

South Tracy and South Black

South Tracy Avenue

N

are its most impressive residences. Virtually all of the south side's historic buildings—with the significant exception of historic buildings on the Montana State University campus—are located in one of five National Register historic districts explored in the following section.

South Tracy and South Black Historic District

THE SOUTH TRACY AND SOUTH BLACK HISTORIC DISTRICT includes some of the first residential areas to develop south of Main Street. Most of today's historic district is located within the original town site platted in 1864; Leander M. Black

*Richard and Mary McDonald constructed the two-story, relatively unadorned home at 308 South Tracy Avenue (**site 71**, right) circa 1872. The McDonalds were freed slaves from Missouri who traveled to Bozeman to escape the South's Jim Crow laws in the aftermath of the Civil War. The frame residence on the left was demolished to build the circa 1884 Vivion home at 304 South Tracy Avenue (**site 70**).* PIONEER MUSEUM

SELECTED SOUTH TRACY AND SOUTH BLACK HISTORIC DISTRICT SITES

W. Babcock St.   E. Babcock St.

63   61

W. Olive St.   E. Olive St.

68   82
69

W. Curtiss St.

70
71

72   73

W. Koch St.

S. Willson Ave.   S. Tracy Ave.   S. Black Ave.   S. Bozeman Ave.

74   E. Koch St.
75
76
                                        66

W. Story St.
77   E. Story St.
78   81
79

80

W. Dickerson St.

E. Dickerson St.

N

platted Black's Addition, south of the original town site and also within today's historic district, in 1871. Home construction began there almost immediately, with the *Avant-Courier* reporting in 1871 that "Black's Addition is becoming the most attractive part of our beautiful City and its rapid improvement is due to the enterprise of Col. L. M. Black."

Any account of the district has to begin with the circa 1872 McDonald Home at 308 South Tracy Avenue (**site 71**) and the twin 1879 Samuel Lewis residences (**sites 68 and 69**, 209 and 211 South Tracy Avenue). Richard and Mary McDonald's vernacular residence recalls the modest I-House dwellings common to the American South throughout the nineteenth century—an architectural influence the McDonalds may have introduced to Bozeman. Lewis built his twin residences for use as rentals; his own 1881 home at 308 South Bozeman Avenue (**site 66**) was substantially remodeled in 1889. This beautifully restored home

SELECTED SOUTH TRACY AND SOUTH BLACK HISTORIC DISTRICT SITES

61. Blackmore Apartment Building, 120 South Black Avenue, 1912
63. St. James Episcopal Church, 5 West Olive Street, 1890
66. Lewis House, 308 South Bozeman Avenue, 1881, remodeled 1889
68. Lewis Rental House, 209 South Tracy Avenue, 1879
69. Lewis Rental House, 211 South Tracy Avenue, 1879
70. Vivion House, 304 South Tracy Avenue, c. 1884
71. McDonald House, 308 South Tracy Avenue, c. 1872
72. Niles House, 315 South Tracy Avenue, 1890
73. Hanly House, 318 South Tracy Avenue, 1892

74. 412 South Tracy Avenue, c. 1906
75. Metheney House, 416 South Tracy Avenue, c. 1910
76. 420 South Tracy Avenue, c. 1907
77. Bunker House, 501 South Tracy Avenue, c. 1914
78. Calloway House, 505 South Tracy Avenue, c. 1914
79. Willson House, 509 South Tracy Avenue, c. 1914
80. Longfellow School, 516 South Tracy Avenue, 1939
81. Bartholomew House, 433 South Black Avenue, c. 1920
82. Nichols House, 301 South Black Avenue, c. 1880

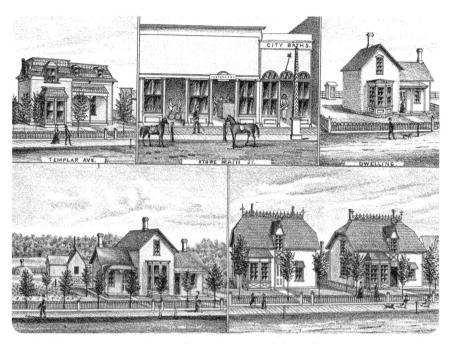

Haitian immigrant Samuel Lewis invested heavily in Bozeman real estate, as demonstrated here by these engravings of his Main Street business, rental properties, and private residence. From Michael Leeson, History of Montana, 1735–1885 *(Chicago, 1885).*

is located east of the historic district on South Bozeman Avenue and echoes the popular Queen Anne style.

The McDonald and Lewis homes reflect the spirit of opportunity and sense of new beginnings that guided many westward. Richard and Mary McDonald were former slaves who traveled to Montana to escape the post–Civil War South. Samuel Lewis was one of the fourteen million immigrants who arrived in the United States between 1820 and 1890. The mixed-race Lewis was born in the West Indies in 1832 and immigrated to New York City while a teenager. In the 1850s and early 1860s, Lewis traveled the West, working as a barber and miner. His barbershop thrived and Lewis proved a shrewd businessman, able to parlay his profits into new investments, including real estate. Two of the rental houses he owned were designed by architect Byron Vreeland (**sites 68 and 69**, 209 and 211 South Tracy Avenue), though 211 South Tracy has been substantially altered. The 1880-era residences stand as reminders of Lewis's contribution to early Bozeman and of the community's multicultural past.

*By the 1880s, development along South Tracy and South Black avenues began to give Bozeman a new air of permanence. The growing wealth of the townspeople is reflected in the circa 1884 two-story, Queen Anne– style Vivion Home at 304 South Tracy Avenue (**site 70**), with its distinctive arched and stained glass windows. The bright red bricks used to build the Vivion residence indicate high iron content and an elevated firing temperature.* AUTHOR

Other early neighborhood residents include George Niles and Ed Hanley, local tinsmiths who profited from the building boom that occurred during the drive for the state capital. Both men built Queen Anne–style homes in the 300 block of South Tracy Avenue (**sites 72 and 73**, 315 and 318 South Tracy Avenue), Niles in 1890 and Hanly in 1892. Hanly's was one of the last houses built in the district before the Panic of 1893 dramatically slowed construction.

When prosperity returned in the early twentieth century, tastes had changed, bringing new architectural styles to Bozeman. The simpler lines of the Colonial Revival and Craftsman styles replaced the complicated angles and exag-

*Built circa 1880 by real estate entrepreneur George Nichols, this large vernacular home at 301 South Black Avenue (**site 82**) was one of the earliest dwellings in the neighborhood.* AUTHOR

*Builder John Bartholomew's own bungalow at 433 South Black Avenue (**site 81**) demonstrates many of the most common elements of the Craftsman style, including a low-pitched gabled roof, triangular knee braces and exposed rafter tails, and a full-width front porch with curved porch supports.* AUTHOR

gerated ornamentation popular in the 1880 and 1890s. While many members of the upper class retained professional architects to design their homes, Bozeman's middle class increasingly turned to home plans available in pattern books. Pattern-book houses became popular and even stylish in the hands of an accomplished builder.

Brothers John A. and Elmer Bartholomew built pattern-book bungalows in neighborhoods all over Bozeman. In the first decade of the twentieth century, John Bartholomew built three houses at 412, 416, and 420 South Tracy Avenue (**sites 74, 75, and 76**). Each features similar Queen Anne–style influences likely derived from the same pattern-book design. Meanwhile, his own residence at 433 South Black Avenue (**site 81**) is one of the best examples of a Craftsman-style bungalow found anywhere in Bozeman. For his part, Elmer Bartholomew joined forces with architect Fred Willson to produce the Colonial Revival–influenced dwellings at 501 and 505 South Tracy Avenue (**sites 77 and 78**) and the gambrel-roofed Dutch Colonial–style home at 509 South Tracy Avenue (**site 79**), which the architect and his family lived in for decades.

Like the Panic of 1893, the Great Depression slowed neighborhood construction to a near standstill, with one exception: the Longfellow School at 516 South Tracy Avenue (**site 80**), built in 1939 and financed with a combination of local bonds and New Deal funds. Designed by Fred Willson in the distinctive Streamlined Moderne style, the neighborhood school is a unifying element in the community.

Lindley Place Historic District

THIS QUIET MIDDLE-CLASS NEIGHBORHOOD was the brainchild of developers Joseph Lindley and John C. Guy, who platted the addition in 1880. Lindley Place sits just two blocks south of the urbanity of Main Street, yet the quarter seems a world apart. No crossroads interrupt Lindley Place, Bozeman Creek bubbles along the eastern portion of the neighborhood, and the broad, grassy expanse of Bogert Park (**site 65**) sits across the creek at South Church Avenue and Bogert Place. Initially the home of the lumberyard and planing mill of Lindley and Guy,

SELECTED LINDLEY PLACE
HISTORIC DISTRICT SITES

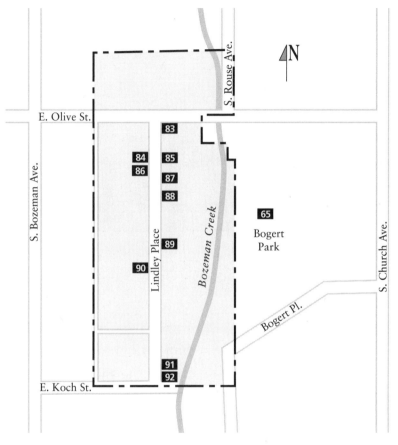

65. Bogert Park, South Church Avenue, purchased
    in 1917 and expanded in 1921
83. Lindley House, 202 Lindley Place, 1892
84. 207 Lindley Place, c. 1883
85. 208 Lindley Place, 1919
86. 211 Lindley Place, c. 1880
87. Mimmack House, 212 Lindley Place, 1919
88. 218 Lindley Place, c. 1886
89. 306 Lindley Place, 1919
90. Highsmith House, 317 Lindley Place, c. 1888
91. 326 Lindley Place, 1913
92. 330 Lindley Place, 1913

*Blacksmith George Highsmith built this Queen Anne–style home at 317 Lindley Place (**site 90**) circa 1888. The house is an embodiment of the prosperity tradesmen such as Highsmith experienced during the boom times of the 1880s.* AUTHOR

the district still contains two shotgun-style homes, 207 and 211 Lindley Place (**sites 84 and 86**), from the neighborhood's early commercial period. These narrow, front-gabled buildings, only one room wide, housed men who labored at the Lindley and Guy lumberyard in the early 1880s.

By the mid-1880s, the neighborhood began to take on a distinctly residential appearance, especially after Joe Lindley built his first home (now demolished) at the intersection of Lindley Place (then Lindley Street) and East Olive Street. Lindley began to sell home lots, and by 1889 eight homes graced the 200 and 300 blocks of Lindley Place.

Typical of these 1880s homes are the residences at 218 and 317 Lindley Place (**sites 88 and 90**). The ornate porch of the former and the asymmetrical massing of the later both reflect the popular Queen Anne style. Joseph Lindley's own notable brick vernacular residence at 202 Lindley Place (**site 83**) was completed in 1892, just before the Panic of 1893.

Bozeman's expanding middle class brought a wave of new construction to the neighborhood in the early twentieth century. These second-generation homes reflect early-twentieth-century home builders' embrace of the Craftsman style. Fine examples of Craftsman-style bungalows can be found in the 200 and 300 blocks of Lindley Place (**sites 85, 87, 89, 91, and 92**). Bozeman builder J. H. Mimmack constructed the bungalows at 326 and 330 Lindley Place (**sites 91 and 92**) in 1913, and the homes combined pattern-book inspiration with the builder's own originality. He completed three more residences immediately following World War I, including his own bungalow at 212 Lindley Place (**site 87**).

Despite the addition of some new residences, the district has changed little since the 1930s. Bozeman Creek, shade trees, and sidewalks imprinted with "Lindley Place—1906" all contribute to the neighborhood's historic character and secluded feel.

Bon Ton Historic District

In 1864, Bozeman co-founder William W. Alderson received title to land just south of Main Street. Eight years later he platted Alderson's Addition, laying out the nine square blocks that today form the northern end of the Bon Ton Historic District. A prolonged economic slump in the 1870s

SELECTED BON TON
HISTORIC DISTRICT SITES

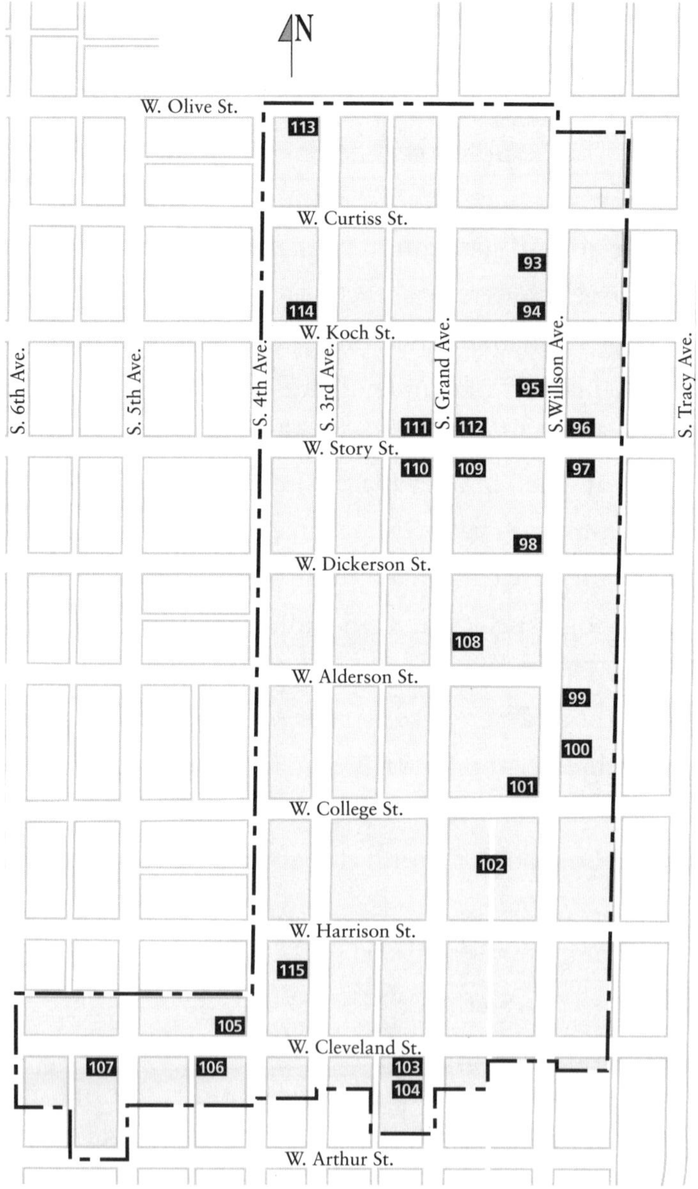

↑N

W. Olive St.

113

W. Curtiss St.

93

114   94

W. Koch St.

95

111 112   96

W. Story St.

110 109   97

98

W. Dickerson St.

108

W. Alderson St.

99

100

101

W. College St.

102

W. Harrison St.

115

105

107   106

W. Cleveland St.

103
104

W. Arthur St.

S. 6th Ave.
S. 5th Ave.
S. 4th Ave.
S. 3rd Ave.
S. Grand Ave.
S. Willson Ave.
S. Tracy Ave.

prevented homebuilding until the arrival of the Northern Pacific Railroad, but in 1883, Alderson's Addition began to take shape. That year, Alderson platted the Fairview Addition south of his original addition. Not to be outdone, Nelson Story headed a group that platted the Park Addition to the west.

South Willson Avenue (named Central Avenue until 1920) traversed the heart of these three additions, and Alderson designed it to be a grand boulevard, twenty feet wider than other local streets. From the beginning, he intended the boulevard to become Bozeman's most fashionable street, a fact recognized by the editor of the *Avant-Courier,* who wrote in 1884 that it was developing "into a Bon Ton residence street in Bozeman." "Bon ton" means "sophisticated," and it remains

SELECTED BON TON HISTORIC DISTRICT SITES

93. Armstrong/Phillips House, 307 South Willson Avenue, 1883
94. Alderson/Chisholm House, 319 South Willson Avenue, 1883
95. Blair House, 415 South Willson Avenue, 1912
96. Fielding House, 420 South Willson Avenue, 1884
97. Willson House, 504 South Willson Avenue, 1886
98. Mendenhall House, 521 South Willson Avenue, 1886
99. Anceney House, 704 South Willson Avenue, 1929
100. Fisher House, 712 South Willson Avenue, 1909
101. King House, 725 South Willson Avenue, 1906
102. T. B. Story Mansion, 811 South Willson Avenue, 1910
103. Sweet House, 1001 South Grand Avenue, 1917
104. Davis House, 1007 South Grand Avenue, 1916
105. Bath House, 405 West Cleveland Avenue, 1927
106. Browning House, 412 West Cleveland Avenue, 1936
107. Graf House, 504 West Cleveland Avenue, c. 1933
108. Clark Apartment Building, 616 South Grand Avenue, 1914
109. Kopp House, 502 South Grand Avenue, c. 1903
110. Lamme/Armstrong House, 501 South Grand Avenue, 1893
111. Martin House, 419 South Grand Avenue, 1892
112. Alderson House, 420 South Grand Avenue, 1900
113. Benepe House, 201 South Third Avenue, 1883
114. Roecher House, 319 South Third Avenue, 1900
115. Cobleigh House, 909 South Third Avenue, 1912

*Matt Alderson's impressive home at 319 South Willson Avenue (**site 94**) was one of the first residences built in his father's new addition. Constructed in 1883, the home incorporates Italianate features, including the style's characteristic low-pitched roof, extended exterior cornice moldings, narrow windows, and wide, overhanging eaves supported by brackets. This house is one of Bozeman's few residential Italianate-influenced homes. The style was already considered old-fashioned in the 1880s.* MOR

the appropriate term to characterize the entire quarter, which boasts one of the finest collections of residential architecture anywhere in Montana.

Local attorney Frank K. Armstrong, along with Alderson's son, Matt, set the tone for the new neighborhood with substantial brick homes influenced by the Italianate style at 307 and 319 South Willson Avenue (**sites 93 and 94**). (Armstrong's

*John Mendenhall's 1886 home at 521 South Willson Avenue (**site 98**) features many of the most common elements of the Queen Anne–style "spindlework," including gable decoration, spindlework porch ornamentation, and a cutaway bay window.* AUTHOR

residence was later remodeled in the Colonial Revival style.) Other noteworthy residences soon followed. The year 1884 saw the construction of what may be Bozeman's first professionally designed home, a Colonial Revival–style residence, the Fielding House, at 420 South Willson Avenue (**site 96**), designed by architect Byron Vreeland. In 1886, Civil War veteran Lester Willson built his own grand Colonial Revival–style home at 504 South Willson Avenue (**site 97**), on the street that would

*Originally built for local butcher John Kopp circa 1903, this home at 502 South Grand Avenue (**site 109**) is one of Bozeman's outstanding architectural gems and is a fine example of the "Free Classic" form of the Queen Anne style.* AUTHOR

later be renamed in his honor. John Mendenhall's expressive spindlework Queen Anne–style home at 521 South Willson Avenue (**site 98**) added another elegant residence to the fashionable avenue that same year. The building of today's Bon Ton district was well under way.

The Bon Ton district saw another surge in residential construction during the early 1890s in conjunction with the bid for the state capital. As the *Bozeman Daily Chronicle* noted during the early 1890s building boom: "The frame house, hast-

*Like the Kopp House, the 1900 Roecher House at 319 South Third Avenue (**site 114**) is a fine example of the "Free Classic" variety of the Queen Anne style. The turret, multi-story bay windows, decorative sunburst within the pedimented porch gable, and classical porch columns are all distinctive elements of the style, a south side favorite during the early twentieth century.* AUTHOR

ily and cheaply built without plaster is no longer the rule, but rather the exception. . . . [A]mong the finer residences is that of J. E. Martin's which will cost fully twenty thousand dollars."

In 1890, the Capitol Hill Addition was platted in today's Bon Ton district, with several streets named for U.S. presidents. The newly created South Grand Avenue was soon home to several fine residences, including the J. E. Martin and Lamme homes at 419 and 501 South Grand Avenue (**sites 111 and 110**). These were the last houses built in the neighborhood before

*In the 1920s, fraternities and sororities purchased many prominent Bon Ton residences. By 1927, eight fraternities and two sororities were located in former private residences on South Willson, South Grand, and South Third Avenues, including the T. B. Story Mansion at 811 South Willson Avenue (**site 102**, pictured here), the Kopp House at 502 South Grand Avenue (**site 109**), and the impressive 1883 Benepe House at 201 South Third Avenue (**site 113**). Only five fraternities remained in this neighborhood by 1954, and today most Greek system residences are located immediately east of the university campus.* AUTHOR

the full effects of the Panic of 1893 interrupted residential construction. As the economy recovered and the new century commenced, the charming 1900 Frank Alderson House was constructed at the corner of South Grand Avenue and West Story Street (**site 112**). These three residences were joined in turn in 1903 by the impressive Kopp House at 502 South Grand Avenue (**site 109**), which combines such Queen Anne–style features as a six-sided turret with such Colonial Revival elements as an elegantly columned front porch. The architecturally fascinating foursome makes this intersection one of the most visually interesting in Bozeman.

The early decades of the twentieth century brought a new wave of construction. At the unrivaled heart of the Bon Ton is the impressive 1910 T. B. Story Mansion/Sigma Alpha Epsilon (SAE) House at 811 South Willson Avenue (**site 102**), attributed to architect C. S. Haire of the firm of Link and Haire, with Fred Willson serving as the on-site construction supervisor. Combining Shingle-style, Stick-style, and Queen Anne–style elements with Classical features, the mansion occupies an entire city block.

Fred Willson designed many of the Bon Ton district's elegant twentieth-century residences. Over time, Willson had mastered a wide range of styles, a useful trait for an architect working during a period when fashion demanded copies of many historical or regional styles. The customer-pleasing architect was as comfortable working in the Mission Revival style—as seen in one of his earliest residential designs, the distinctive 1909 Fisher House at 712 South Willson Avenue (**site 100**)— as in the Colonial Revival style, which inspired his design for the 1912 Blair House at 415 South Willson Avenue (**site 95**).

Both the Mission style and the Colonial Revival style looked to America's past for architectural inspiration, but Willson also turned to European models. Willson's 1929 design for the Tudor Revival–style Anceney House at 704 South Willson Avenue (**site 99**) made reference to the architecture of English country homes. His 1927 Mediterranean Revival–style Bath House at 405 West Cleveland Avenue (**site 105**) and his circa

*The 1912 Blair House at 415 South Willson Avenue (**site 95**) displays many of the design elements common to the Colonial Revival style. The decorative cornice, elliptical fanlight over the centrally located front entrance, and porch with classical columns are all hallmarks of the style, which celebrates the country's colonial past.* AUTHOR

1933 Graf House at 504 West Cleveland Avenue (**site 107**), with its signature copper mansard roof, also reflected European traditions. Yet not all of Willson's designs looked backward. In 1936, for example, he designed the decidedly modern Browning House at 412 West Cleveland Avenue (**site 106**). One of Bozeman's few International-style homes, it features the style's defining flat roof, unadorned walls, and asymmetrical façade.

During the first three decades of the twentieth century, newly successful businessmen sought residences along the tony avenues of Bon Ton neighborhoods. The Craftsman style was the dominant home type built throughout Bozeman during that era. Good examples include the 1912 Fred Willson–designed Cobleigh House at 909 South Third Avenue (**site 115**) and the distinctive stone- and concrete-clad Clark Apartment Building at 616 South Grand Avenue (**site 108**). Completed in 1914, the Clark is one of Bozeman's few historic buildings constructed entirely of concrete blocks. Built side by side in the Bon Ton district, the 1917 Sweet House at 1001 South Grand Avenue (**site 103**) and the 1916 Davis House at 1007 South Grand Avenue (**site 104**) are two more fine examples of the Craftsman style.

The presence of the Montana Agricultural College helped offset the most devastating effects of the Great Depression,

*The 1909 Mission-style Fisher House at 712 South Willson Avenue (**site 100**), shown here before mature landscaping replaced the open prairie, is one of the few of its type in Bozeman and represents one of Fred Willson's earliest residential designs.* MOR

*The false half-timbering on the 1929 Anceney House at 704 South Willson Avenue (**site 99**) emulates the structural timbered framework common to medieval homes.* AUTHOR

and by the late 1930s most of the Bon Ton's historically significant homes had been built. In 1935, the City of Bozeman installed elegant concrete lamp posts along South Willson and West Cleveland Avenues. Today, the lamp posts—the only remaining original lamp posts located in a Bozeman historic neighborhood—help define southern and eastern borders of this impressive National Register district.

The 1908 Fisher residence (top photo), an extraordinary Tudor Revival–style home, was demolished to make way for the construction of the Sigma Chi fraternity house in 1961. At the time, communities often viewed older residences as antiquated eyesores rather than valuable reminders of a city's layered past. Fortunately, the stately 1906 King residence at 725 South Willson Avenue (**site 101,** bottom photo), which combines both Queen Anne and Colonial Revival elements, still graces the south side. MOR

SELECTED SOUTH TRACY AVENUE HISTORIC DISTRICT SITES

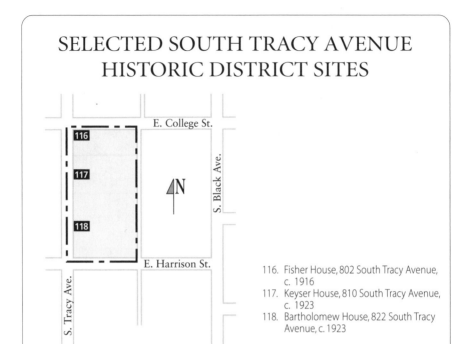

116. Fisher House, 802 South Tracy Avenue, c. 1916
117. Keyser House, 810 South Tracy Avenue, c. 1923
118. Bartholomew House, 822 South Tracy Avenue, c. 1923

South Tracy Avenue Historic District

THE SOUTH TRACY AVENUE HISTORIC DISTRICT IS a small group of homes with their own history that lies just one block east of the Bon Ton district. These bungalow-inspired homes occupy the Butte Addition, platted in 1890 as part of Bozeman's unsuccessful bid for the state capital, but little development occurred here until the mid-1910s. That early isolation is the foundation of the historic significance of the neighborhood. Surrounded by residences of later construction, this group of homes is clearly defined and today retains a visual coherence that denotes the period in which the homes were built.

The district's oldest residence is the Fisher House at 802 South Tracy (**site 116**). Built circa 1916, its design is attributed to Charles Fisher's brother-in-law, Fred Willson. For the district's remaining residences, the carpenters followed Willson's lead, adapting the general pattern of this Craftsman-style bungalow, but with less elaboration.

In the later 1910s and early 1920s, a group of local builders—William C. Smith, Elmer Bartholomew, George M. Wimmer, and Guy A. Ensinger—bought lots and began to build homes for resale, often living in the houses until they sold. For example, the prolific Bartholomew, who built the bungalow at 822 South Tracy Avenue (**site 118**), also constructed the house at 810 South Tracy Avenue (**site 117**), where he resided for a few years following its completion circa 1923. It is the last home built in the district. Open fields lay to the south and west of the little neighborhood until the late 1940s, when postwar residential construction began.

Cooper Park Historic District

ALTHOUGH NELSON STORY, JOHN S. DICKERSON, and Walter Cooper platted the Park Addition, west of today's Bon Ton district, in 1883, the area remained an open plain into the late 1890s. By 1904, only two Cooper Park blocks (West Olive and West Story between South Fourth and Fifth avenues) had more than five houses. Between 1900 and 1920, however, Bozeman grew from 3,419 people to 6,183 people, and construction in Cooper Park boomed as builders sought to provide affordable homes for the growing middle class.

Listings for local builders in the Bozeman *Polk City Directory* effectively demonstrate the new growth. The 1910 city directory lists only nine local builders; by 1916, that number

SELECTED COOPER PARK
HISTORIC DISTRICT SITES

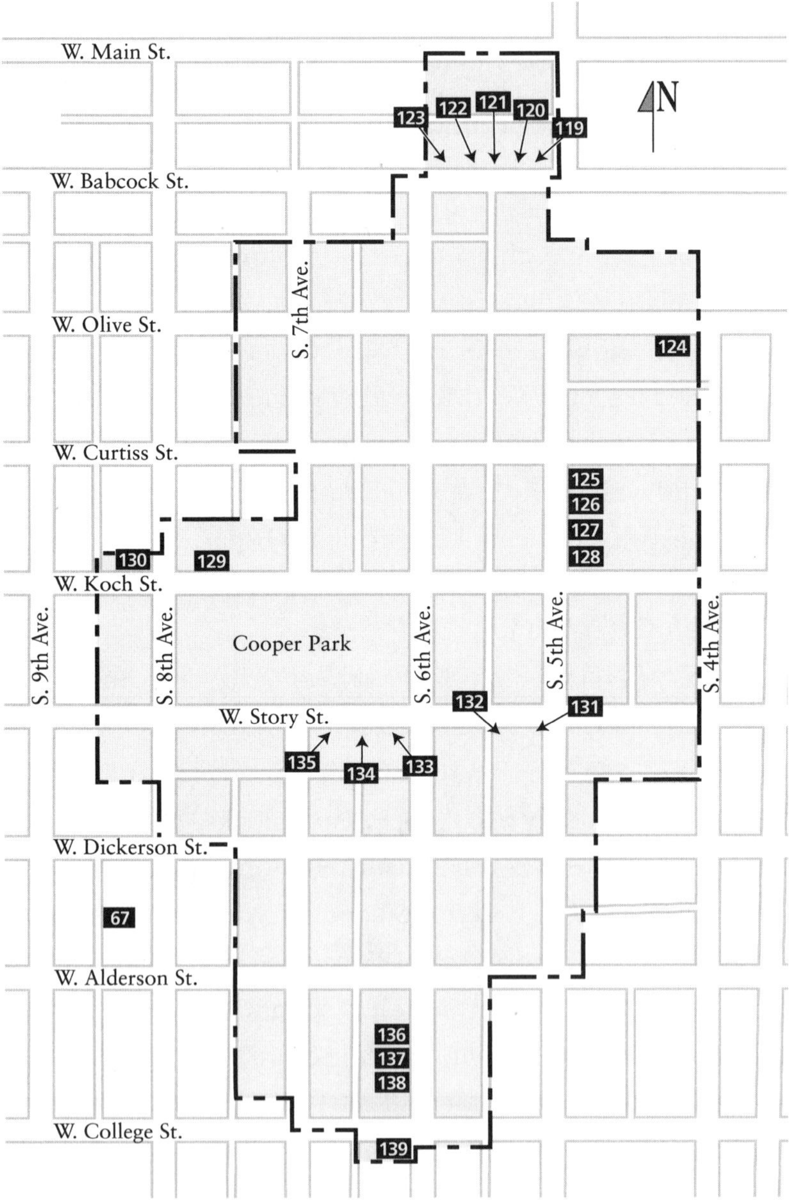

W. Main St.

123 122 121 120

119

N

W. Babcock St.

S. 7th Ave.

W. Olive St.

124

W. Curtiss St.

125
126
127
128

130 129

W. Koch St.

S. 9th Ave.

S. 8th Ave.

Cooper Park

S. 6th Ave.

S. 5th Ave.

S. 4th Ave.

132 131

W. Story St.

135 134 133

W. Dickerson St.

67

W. Alderson St.

136
137
138

W. College St.

139

had grown to twenty-three. Several of these men—Elmer Bartholomew, William H. Cline, Guy A. Ensinger, and Lou Sievert—were particularly active in the Cooper Park area, constructing groups of similar homes for resale. These builders primarily relied on pattern books like Fred Hodgson's *Practical Bungalows and Cottages for Town and Country,* which offered plans for all budgets and tastes. Such books contained perspective drawings and floor plans and detailed working plans could be ordered for as little as five dollars.

While pattern books featured styles from Queen Anne to Tudor Revival, the Craftsman-style bungalow was the era's most popular house type. In the United States, the fashionable style gathered momentum during the first decade of the twentieth century and remained popular well into the 1920s. Bungalow floor plans maximized the usefulness of every square inch while dormers converted attics into living space. Such innovations made these homes attractive and affordable.

SELECTED COOPER PARK
HISTORIC DISTRICT SITES

67. Irving School, 611 South Eighth Avenue, 1939
119. 507 West Babcock Street, c. 1910
120. 511 West Babcock Street, c. 1910
121. 515 West Babcock Street, c. 1909
122. 519 West Babcock Street, c. 1911
123. 523 West Babcock Street, c. 1911
124. 412 West Olive Street, pre-1904
125. 308 South Fifth Avenue, c. 1917
126. 314 South Fifth Avenue, c. 1917
127. 316 South Fifth Avenue, c. 1917
128. 320 South Fifth Avenue, c. 1917

129. 715 West Koch Street, c. 1918
130. 321 South Eighth Avenue, c. 1919
131. 502 West Story Street, c. 1930
132. 510 West Story Street, c. 1930
133. Purdum House, 602 West Story Street, c. 1914
134. 612 West Story Street, 1932
135. Chambers House, 616 West Story Street, 1932
136. 715 South Sixth Avenue, c. 1915
137. 719 South Sixth Avenue, c. 1916
138. 721 South Sixth Avenue, c. 1916
139. 807 South Sixth Avenue, c. 1920

No. 1096

PRICE
of Plans and
Specifications
$5.00

HOUSE DESIGN No. 1096

Full and complete working plans and specifications of this house will be furnished for $5.00.
Cost of this house is from $1,250 to $1,500 according to the locality in which it is built.

FLOOR PLAN OF DESIGN No. 1096

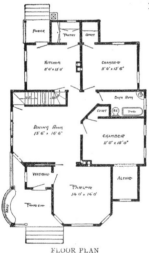

FLOOR PLAN

SIZE
Width, 33 feet.
Length, 50 feet.

Blue prints consist of foundation plan; floor plan; front, rear,
two side elevations; wall sections and all necessary interior details.
Specifications consist of about fifteen pages of typewritten matter.

*Often builders working in the Cooper Park area used mass-produced
floor plans, adapting them to the site or customer taste, but in the case
of the Queen Anne–inspired cottage at 412 West Olive Street (site 124),
few adjustments were necessary. The home's original plan corresponded
almost perfectly with Hodgson's "House Design No. 1096," shown here.
From Fred T. Hodgson,* Practical Bungalows and Cottages for Town
and Country *(Chicago, 1915).*

*Constructed circa 1916 by Guy Ensinger, the bungalows at 719 and 721 South Sixth Avenue (**sites 137 and 138**) are near replicas of each other. Fred Hodgson's Practical Bungalows and Cottages for Town and Country alone provided local builders like Ensinger with over three hundred houses to choose from. Most of the homes in the book were estimated to cost between seven hundred and three thousand dollars to construct. Blueprints, drawn en masse by architects, included side/rear, floor, roof, and foundations plans, and were priced between five and ten dollars.* AUTHOR

William Cline built several bungalows on the 300 block of South Fifth Avenue circa 1917, filling much of the entire east side of the block with the small, closely spaced homes (**sites 125–128**). The cluster of five houses that Elmer Bartholomew constructed between 1909 and 1911 on the north side of the 500 block of West Babcock Street (**sites 119–123**) includes some of his best work. The strong influence of the Craftsman style shows in the homes' fully recessed porches and single front dormers.

Like his productive brother Elmer, builder John Bartholomew constructed compact bungalows in Cooper Park neighborhoods. The circa 1920 residence at 807 South Sixth

Avenue (**site 139**) demonstrates some of the small liberties that the Bartholomew brothers and other local builders took with pattern book homes, such as the decorative additions of Tudoresque false-timbering and curved porch columns.

Guy Ensinger continued the pattern of bungalow homes when he completed three residences on South Sixth Avenue (**sites 136, 137, and 139**) just before America's entry into World War I. Ensinger's work earned the praise of *American Builder* magazine, which called the homes "practical and economical"—the very type of residence Ensinger and his colleagues sought to construct.

The 1930s saw a growing number of simple one-story houses with little detailing—a reflection of the nation's economic woes

Fred Willson designed the Craftsman-style Purdum residence at 602 West Story Street (site 133) circa 1914. It is one of the few architect-designed houses in the Cooper Park district. AUTHOR

In 1932, Fred Willson added the Chateauesque-style Chambers House (site 135) to 616 West Story Street. Its proximity to Cooper Park evokes a decidedly country feel, which complements the residence's bucolic design. AUTHOR

and the rise of no-frills modernism. Cooper Park examples come from builder Lou Sievert, whose compact homes at 502 and 510 West Story Street (**sites 131 and 132**) demonstrate the simplicity of Depression Era architecture.

A few architect-designed houses grace the neighborhood. Three houses Fred Willson designed located directly across the street from Cooper Park showcase the architect's versatility. His circa 1914 Purdum House at 602 West Story Street (**site 133**) offers a distinctive interpretation of the Craftsman style. Willson added two homes to the neighborhood in 1932: the French Eclectic–style Chambers House at 616 West Story Street (**site 135**) and the Colonial Revival–style home located next door at 612 West Story Street (**site 134**). These two homes are also unique for the date of their construction. Built at the beginning of the Great Depression, they deviate from the extreme simplicity of other residences constructed in the Cooper Park district during that era.

Later additions to the neighborhood trace to John D. Wherling, who built bungalows almost exclusively. He left a career in law enforcement—he was the chief of the Bozeman Police Department—and took up residential construction during the years when the post–World War I demand for inexpensive housing was high. Wherling's Cooper Park contributions include one-and-one-half-story bungalows at 321 South Eighth Avenue (**site 130**) and 715 West Koch Street (**site 129**).

Historic Buildings of Montana State University

THE EFFECT OF THE UNIVERSITY on the economic growth of Bozeman and the physical development of the south side is inestimable. Founded in 1893, the school has educated generations of professionals and has served as the technological center for agricultural science throughout the state, developing new crops and directing New Deal farm programs during the lean years of the 1920s and 1930s.

The idea of land-grant colleges dates back to the Civil War, when Congress passed the Morrill Land Grant Act that gave states 6.3 million acres of federal lands to create and support at least one college per state. Ostensibly designed to promote the educational fields of science, classical studies, agriculture, and engineering, the act also promoted the western states' allegiance to the Union during the war-torn 1860s.

SELECTED MONTANA STATE
UNIVERSITY SITES

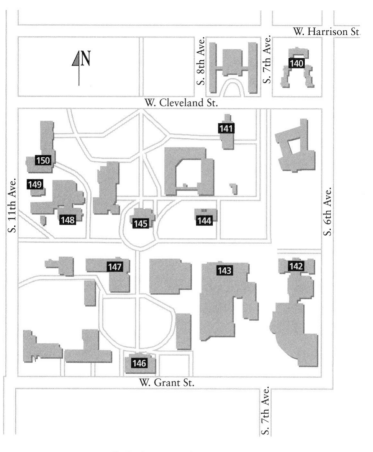

140. Alfred Atkinson Quadrangle, 1935
141. Herrick Hall, 1926
142. Roberts Hall, 1922
143. Strand Student Union, 1940
144. Hamilton Hall, 1910
145. Montana Hall, 1896
146. Romney Gymnasium, 1922
147. Reid Hall, 1959
148. Lewis Hall, 1923
149. Taylor Hall, 1896
150. Linfield Hall, 1909

*Completed just before Montana Hall (**site 145**) in 1896, Taylor Hall (**site 149**) is the oldest campus building. Its role as the collegiate home of agricultural study and experimentation is reflected in its barn-like design, complete with gambrel roof.* AUTHOR

Statehood came to Montana in 1889, and four years later Bozeman was awarded the Agricultural College of the State of Montana. Founded on February 16, 1893, the school at first existed only on paper. There was no campus, and the first fourteen students attended classes in the vacant rooms of an existing school building. Later classes moved to an old roller-skating rink that had become a private school, the Bozeman Academy, which then stood on the grounds of today's Holy Rosary Church on West Main Street (**site 4**). In 1896, the school's first year on campus, 139 students enrolled for a ten-dollar fee.

By 1896, construction of Taylor Hall (**site 149**) was well under way. Designed by the college's first president, Augustus Ryon, to house the State Agricultural Experiment Station, it is the campus's oldest building. The experiment station's various farm buildings sat in the vicinity of today's Cheever and Haynes halls. That same year, masons laid the cornerstone for Montana Hall (**site 145**), whose signature cupola rises high into the Big Sky. State architect John C. Paulson designed the building, which displays elements of the Romanesque Revival style in its decorative belt coursing, gabled parapet over the arched entrance, and rusticated stone foundation.

More construction followed, and the new buildings especially reflected the importance of agriculture to the college's mission. Constructed in 1909 through a special legislative grant of eighty thousand dollars, Linfield Hall (**site 150**) was originally named Morrill Hall after the legislation that established the land-grant college system. The college renamed the building for Frederick B. Linfield, the dean of agriculture and experiment station director from 1913 to 1937. Designed by the architectural firm of Link and Haire, the Classical Revival building displays many of the key elements of the style, including a pedimented central bay with centrally located window, pedimented dormers, decorative keystones above the entrances, and an accented cornice with dentil molding.

In 1910, Fred Willson—then just beginning his career— designed Hamilton Hall (**site 144**) to house female students. The building displays classic elements of the Mission Revival style, including the shaped roof parapet and recessed central bay with projecting side bays. Though the building was new,

*Early college campus buildings were constructed in relative isolation from the rest of Bozeman. Hamilton Hall, built in 1910 (**site 144**, left, multi-story), was named for Emma Hamilton, wife of the college's third president, James Hamilton, who successfully resisted plans to merge the college with the one in Missoula. In the center is the unmistakable profile of Montana Hall (**site 145**), constructed in 1896.* PIONEER MUSEUM

the presence of women on the campus was not. Women had attended the college since its second year of existence. As a dormitory, Hamilton Hall remained a center of campus social life well into the mid-twentieth century.

While the development of the campus is more generally associated with Fred Willson, it was architect Cass Gilbert who completed the campus master plan in 1919. Based in St. Paul, Minnesota, and later New York City, Gilbert was a nationally renowned architect. A pioneer in skyscraper design, Gilbert created the 1909 Woolworth Building in New York City, then the tallest building in the world. Gilbert later capped his career by designing the U.S. Supreme Court Building in Washington, D.C.

*The brick buildings of the Alfred Atkinson Quadrangle (**site 140**) are the only campus structures financed by 1930s federal public works programs because college president Alfred Atkinson generally opposed such New Deal programs.* AUTHOR

Known for his approach to civic design, Gilbert had previously developed master plans for the University of Texas and Oberlin College. His plan for the Bozeman campus incorporated the few existing buildings into a cohesive design for long-term development. Though difficult to discern today, elements of the Gilbert plan included a central oval flanked by "quads" of academic buildings and connected by vehicular and pedestrian pathways. As time passed, successive college administrations departed from the Gilbert plan.

The 1920s were a busy time for campus construction. The Romney Gymnasium (**site 146**), Roberts Hall (**site 142**), and Lewis Hall (**site 148**) were completed by 1923, and Herrick Hall (**site 141**) was constructed in 1926. Designed by Fred Willson, Roberts Hall displays elements of the Romanesque Revival style in its gabled entrance and arched doors and contrasting stone belt courses as well as its decorative features, such as the stone medallions that flank the main entrance and copper coping along the parapet roof. Lewis Hall is named for Meriwether Lewis, and murals inside the building highlight Lewis and Clark's trek across the West. Herrick Hall, meanwhile, is named to honor Una Herrick, the college's first dean of women. Recently, it has been the subject of extensive preservation and restoration efforts.

During the 1930s, Fred Willson and G. G. Cottier completed two substantial campus buildings. The 1935 Alfred Atkinson Quadrangle (**site 140**) offered a new option for female stu-

*The 1959 Reid Hall (**site 147**) is a dramatic departure from earlier campus architecture. Influenced by the International style of the 1930s, this type of no-frills architecture emphasized pragmatism and progress in the use of glass, flat roofs, rectangular plans, and the rejection of nonessential decoration. The style dominated American institutional and commercial architecture from the 1950s through the late 1970s.* AUTHOR

dents who desired to live on campus. A 1935 edition of the campus newspaper noted the "convenience of central kitchen service," which made the dormitories the "only ones of their kind in the United States." The Student Union (now the Strand Student Union) began in 1915 as a simple thirty-two-by-thirty-five-foot log cabin. Students continued to congregate in the cabin until a new building was completed in 1940 (**site 143**). Additions to the building in 1957 and 1968 reflect the growth of the university as a whole.

College president Roland Renne expanded the campus during his tenure to meet the post–World War II demand for secondary education. In 1954, he persuaded the Montana Board of Education to authorize a $4.5-million bond issue to construct dormitories. He was able to expand the boundaries of the campus a full mile to the west and one-half mile to the south. Reid Hall (**site 147**), a major instructional and office building, was completed in 1959.

Since Renne's tenure, change and expansion have continued. In 1965, the college's name changed to Montana State University, and new research opportunities, apart from teaching, began to expand the role of school. The 1970s saw the construction of the Reno H. Sales Stadium and a new health and physical education center. More recent large-scale additions to the campus include the state-of-the-art Engineering and Physical Sciences Building. The continuing development of the campus has paralleled Bozeman's own growth. As Bozeman's largest employer, the university has contributed more to Bozeman's development over the past several decades than any other economic or social factor.

BOZEMAN'S OTHER HISTORIC PLACES

Sunset Hills Cemetery is located along East Main Street, adjacent to Lindley Park. British aristocrat William Blackmore purchased the land that became the cemetery in 1872 after his wife, Mary, died in the home of Lester Willson during a western tour. The Blackmores had apparently agreed not to return the other's body home if either one of them died on their trip, so "Lord" Blackmore, as he was mistakenly addressed by admiring locals, purchased five acres of land to create the cemetery—both as a final resting place for his wife and as a gift to show his appreciation for Bozeman's hospitality.

Lady Blackmore's grave joined many others on this hillside, which Bozeman families had used as an informal cemetery since 1867. (Some headstones show even earlier dates, but those mark the graves of people re-interred here in the late nineteenth century.) Town founders John Bozeman, Daniel Rouse, and William Beall are buried here, as is Samuel Lewis, the West Indies immigrant responsible for early Bozeman residences that grace south side neighborhoods. The cemetery includes the well-marked graves of the prominent Story, Willson, and Alderson families as well as the unmarked graves of Chinese

Sunset Hills Cemetery serves as the final resting place for many notables in Bozeman's history. The marble columns flanking the Story family plot once graced the entry to the Nelson Story Mansion on West Main Street. AUTHOR

immigrants and poor-farm inmates. A walk through the cemetery brings into focus Bozeman's diversity, and the average people, infamous personalities, and prominent citizens who shaped the town. Thus, it makes a fitting end to a tour of the city's history.

PRESERVING
BOZEMAN

HOW DOES THE BOZEMAN OF TODAY preserve and interpret all of this history? And why is it important to do so? Like the city's history, Bozeman's historic preservation program did not develop in a vacuum. Instead, Bozeman's preservation-minded citizens were influenced by a growing, nationwide movement to protect and preserve their historic structures.

Nationally, the modern preservation movement began in response to massive federal construction projects, such as the construction of reclamation projects and the interstate highway system that destroyed locally valued historic sites. It grew as the costs of Urban Renewal—a 1960s program designed to reinvigorate urban areas by demolishing supposedly dilapidated older buildings—became clear. In the name of Urban Renewal, cities compromised their historic streetscapes and destroyed thousands of architecturally notable buildings.

It was in this atmosphere that Congress passed the National Historic Preservation Act (NHPA) in 1966. The act authorized the National Park Service to create the National Register of Historic Places and to establish criteria by which to judge a place's local, state, and national historical significance. The

National Register is much more than simply an honor roll of important prehistoric and historic places. Above all, the National Register program seeks to foster a greater understanding of history through the preservation of significant places and by supporting public and private efforts to preserve historical resources nationwide.

What does all this mean for Bozeman? Just as in other places, Bozeman has lost outstanding architectural treasures. Depression Era federal projects meant the demolition of the Nelson Story Mansion and the first county courthouse. Urban Renewal–era demolitions cost the community the 1890 City Hall and Opera House and the 1889 Tilton Building. An under-appreciation for historic buildings meant additional losses to Bozeman's architectural fabric when, for example, the 1882 Tracy Mansion and the 1908 Fisher Mansion were torn down in the 1960s to make way for new construction.

Still, there were voices for preservation. Prominent among them was John N. DeHaas, longtime professor of architectural history at Montana State University. As a teacher, DeHaas ingrained a preservationist ethic in the thousands of students he mentored over the course of his long career. Beginning in the early 1960s, DeHaas recorded many of the first buildings evaluated in Montana as part of the Historic American Building Survey (HABS), a National Park Service program. In 1969, he helped found the state's earliest private preservation organization, the Montana Ghost Town Preservation Society. A critical figure in introducing a preservation ethic to Bozeman, he was a driving force behind the creation of Bozeman's first historic district, the South Willson Historic District (later the

Bon Ton Historic District), listed in the National Register of Historic Places in 1978.

The powerful advocacy and expertise of people like John DeHaas contributed to the growing awareness of historic preservation as a quality-of-life issue. The Bozeman community embraced the idea, and by the mid-1980s, dozens of volunteers had surveyed more than four thousand properties to determine their eligibility for listing in the National Register. They ultimately listed over forty individually significant properties and nearly eight hundred additional properties, most of which contribute to one of Bozeman's nine historic districts.

Today, much of Bozeman is located within the city's Neighborhood Conservation overlay district, formed in 1990. One of the largest in the country, the overlay district serves to protect places located outside of Bozeman's historic core and to preserve for the future the possibility of creating new historic districts. Outside the overlay district, work remains to be done. No Montana State University buildings are listed in the National Register of Historic Places, for example, despite the campus's clear social, economic, and architectural significance. Listing the campus's historic structures should be a priority, as it would signal the university's commitment to historic preservation and provide recognition to an important Bozeman resource. Over the years, Montana State University's Museum of the Rockies research team has generated a tremendous amount of archeological data from the Fort Ellis site that illuminates life at the fort and in early Bozeman. Unfortunately, due to the lack of funding and staff, research related to Fort Ellis is currently dormant.

Off campus, historic preservation is a responsibility shared among citizens, citizen boards, and local government. Citizens work hard to maintain the historic integrity of their homes and businesses. Developers are increasingly respectful of historic surroundings when designing new projects. The city honors property owners and developers who make significant contributions to local historic preservation efforts at Bozeman's annual "Excellence in Historic Preservation" awards event, hosted by the Bozeman Historic Preservation Advisory Board (BHPAB).

The BHPAB serves in an advisory capacity to the City of Bozeman's Historic Preservation Office (within the Bozeman Office of Planning and Community Development) and the Bozeman City Commission. Established in 1985, the board helps carry out local preservation education, integrates historic preservation into local, state, and federal planning efforts, and evaluates and advocates for the stewardship of local historical resources. Its recent victories include persuading the city to purchase the T. B. Story Mansion/SAE House in 2004 with the goal of securing a future for the building that will preserve its historic integrity.

All in all, Bozeman is home to one of the most progressive municipal historic preservation programs in the nation. Two essential ideas lie behind Bozeman's historic preservation program: to educate the public about the breadth of history represented in the community's heritage sites and to preserve these special places for the use and enjoyment of future generations. Funding this guide and the rescue of the T. B. Story Mansion are just two recent examples of ways the preservation community engages in this important work.

RESIDENTIAL ARCHITECTURAL STYLES

by Martha Kohl

STYLE IS ONLY ONE FACTOR that determines a building's appearance—the building's purpose, the financial resources of its owner, and available material are others. But because fashion is ever changing, architectural style provides a useful clue for anyone who wants to guess when a neighborhood developed or a home was constructed. Here are a few facts you'll want to know before exploring Bozeman's residential neighborhoods.

Many houses—particularly working-class homes—are more functional than stylish. Architectural historians tend to refer to them by their shape (an I-House, for example, or a hipped-roof cottage). Nevertheless, after mass production made trimwork more affordable, builders frequently ornamented many smaller late-nineteenth-century homes with some combination of gingerbread, turned porch supports, decorative brackets, and stained glass. Known as Folk Victorian homes or Queen Anne cottages, these working-class residences were generally constructed before the turn of the century.

TYPICAL QUEEN ANNE DETAILS

1) Irregular roofline/floor plan
2) Towers, turrets
3) Wraparound porches
4) Fancy trim
5) Decorative porch posts and spindles

Larger, more complicated Queen Anne–style homes set the fashion for their Folk Victorian emulators, but in addition to gingerbread and turned porch supports, high-style Queen Anne houses usually boasted a jumble of angles and textures. Complex rooflines, turrets, wraparound porches, projecting bays, spindlework, and decorative siding are all marks of a Queen Anne–style home (good local examples include the Lehrkind Mansion at 719 North Wallace Avenue and the Mendenhall House at 521 South Willson Avenue, **sites 46 and 98**). The style was at the height of its popularity between 1880 and 1900.

A second, more conservative style popular in the last quarter of the nineteenth century was Colonial Revival, which grew in popularity following the nation's 1876 centennial celebrations. The style's key characteristics include multiple columns, pedimented porticos, decorative cornices and cornice brackets, pedimented dormers, and doors with fanlights and sidelights. A Colonial Revival home will often feature either a side-gabled or hipped roof and a symmetrical façade. Subtypes include Dutch Colonial (which features distinctive gambrel, or barn-shaped, roofs) and Georgian Revival (distinguished by strict symmetry). Good examples of both of these subtypes include Fred Willson's home in the South Tracy and South Black Historic District, 509 South Tracy Avenue (**site 79**), and the Blair House, 415 South Willson Avenue (**site 95**) in the Bon Ton Historic District.

As the twentieth century approached, home builders increasingly embraced the simpler, more conservative lines of Colonial Revival over the flamboyance of Queen Anne. But before builders abandoned the Queen Anne style altogether, a "Free Classic" subtype of the style emerged. These transitional homes typically featured the classical columns and simpler lines of the Colonial Revival style and the asymmetrical façade of the Queen Anne (see the Kopp House at 502 South Grand Avenue, **site 109**, and the Roecher House at 319 South Third Avenue, **site 114**).

After the turn of the century, Colonial Revival—which remained popular into the 1950s—was joined by other styles that combined "structural simplicity, balanced proportions, and minimal decoration," as architectural historian Clifford

TYPICAL COLONIAL REVIVAL DETAILS

1) Entrance portico
2) Scrolled or broken pediments
3) Sidelights or fanlights
4) Pediments without supporting pilasters
5) Pediment or portico with curved underside
6) Accentuated front doors

Edward Clark aptly described them. Most prominent among them was the Craftsman style, which emphasized the use of natural materials (wood and stone) and honest, efficient design. The style—at its height of popularity in the 1910s—had an ideological edge. Its characteristic low-pitched roofs (intended to help homes blend into their environment) and full-length open porches were thought to connect homeowners to nature. The style's relatively minimal decoration emphasized craftsmanship over ornamentation, a response to twentieth-century anxieties over the changes industrialization had wrought on the country's character. The style's influence extended far beyond its high-style examples at the Beall Park Community Center at 409 North Bozeman Avenue, the Bartholomew House at 433 South Black Avenue, and the

TYPICAL CRAFTSMAN DETAILS

1) Wide, overhanging eaves
2) Exposed rafters
3) Heavy squared columns or porch supports
4) Brackets and braces
5) Gentle roofs with broad gables

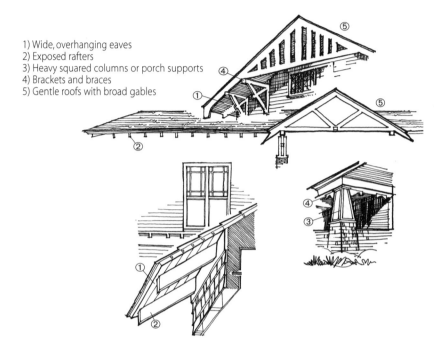

Purdum House at 602 West Story Street (**sites 32, 81, and 133**). Many pattern-book homes and early-twentieth-century bungalows incorporated Craftsman-style elements, including exposed rafter tails, tapered (battered) porch supports, decorative brackets under the eaves, and gable or shed dormers.

The end of World War I saw renewed enthusiasm for period revival styles, especially in architect-designed homes. The war itself was partly responsible; the record number of soldiers serving in Europe meant that more Americans than ever saw European architecture firsthand. The embrace of historical styles was also a conservative reaction to the Roaring Twenties. Homebuyers sought comfort in styles that evoked supposedly simpler times.

Perhaps the most popular period style was the Tudor Revival, inspired by sixteenth- and seventeenth-century English country homes. Steeply pitched roofs, overlapping gables, decorative half timbering, and multi-paned windows characterize the style (see, for example, the Anceney House, **site 99**, at 704 South Willson Avenue). Other revival styles found in Bozeman include Mission (inspired by the Spanish missions of the Southwest; see the Fisher House, **site 100**, 712 South Willson Avenue); Chateauesque (inspired by the monumental chateaus of sixteenth-century France; see the Chambers House, **site 135**, 616 West Story Street); and, of course, Colonial Revival.

BOZEMAN TIME LINE

Paleo-Indian Period (circa 13,000 B.C.–7900 B.C.) Beginning of the peopling of North and South America.

Late Prehistoric Period (circa 500–1700 A.D.) Formation of tribes into today's recognized cultural groups.

Protohistoric Period (circa 1700–1805) Horses, guns, and other trade goods transform tribal life.

1805–06 Lewis and Clark Expedition traverses the region.

1810 John Colter leads a group of fur trappers west over the Bozeman Pass.

Late 1830s Changes in European fashions lead to a decline in the fur trade.

1851 Treaty of Fort Laramie designates the Gallatin Valley as Blackfeet land.

1861–65 Civil War

1862 Montana gold rush begins. Gallatin City established. Congress passes Morrill Land Grant Act, which authorizes the establishment of land-grant colleges throughout the country.

1863 John Bozeman and John Jacobs scout cutoff to the Montana goldfields through territory set aside by treaty as Indian hunting grounds.

1864 Upper East Gallatin Society meets at Jacobs' Crossing to plan the original Bozeman town site. Residents construct first log buildings along Main Street.

1865 Perry and William McAdow construct McAdow Mill in Bozeman.

1866 Nelson Story arrives on the upper Yellowstone River from Texas, completing his epic cattle drive; Red Cloud's War forces permanent closure of the Bozeman Trail.

1867 John Bozeman is killed; the U.S. Army establishes Fort Ellis.

1869 Nation's first transcontinental railroad, the Union Pacific, is completed at Promontory Point, Utah.

1872 Construction of Main Street's Cooper/Black Block is completed; Yellowstone National Park is established.

1876–77 Great Sioux War.

1877 First West Side School is constructed.

1880 Bozeman population reaches nearly 900; new town structures include the Lamme Block and the original county courthouse designed by Byron Vreeland.

1883 The Northern Pacific transcontinental line is completed through Bozeman; Bozeman incorporates.

1886 The U.S. Army abandons Fort Ellis.

1888 The Nelson Story Mansion is completed.

1889 Montana is admitted to the Union as the forty-first state. Bozeman begins its campaign to become the state capital.

1893 Bozeman is awarded the land-grant Agricultural College of the State of Montana, along with the State Agricultural Experiment Station.

1898 The Spanish-American War begins.

1900 Bozeman population reaches 3,419.

1902 The Carnegie Library and Gallatin County High School are constructed.

1906 First Sweet Pea Carnival is held in Bozeman

1909 Gallatin Valley Electric Railway Company establishes the interurban rail system.

1910 Bozeman population is 5,107. Gallatin Canyon route to Yellowstone National Park is completed, establishing the foundation of Bozeman's ties to tourism.

1911 Fred Willson designs the Gallatin County Jail. Chicago, Milwaukee & St. Paul Railroad arrives in Bozeman.

1911–12 Gallatin Valley emerges as the nation's top producer of seed peas.

1916 The United States enters World War I; Bozeman Canning Company is formed.

1919–20 Drought affects much of Montana, forcing thousands of homesteaders from their farms and ranches. The 1920 census records 6,183 people living in Bozeman.

1921 Bozeman adopts a city manager form of government.

1929 Nelson Story passes away in Los Angeles, his primary residence for several years.

1930 The Great Depression begins to affect the nation; Bozeman population is at nearly 7,000.

1936 Federal New Deal funding supports construction of the new Gallatin County Courthouse, designed by Fred Willson.

1940 Bozeman population reaches 8,665.

1941 United States enters World War II; National Guard Armory is constructed downtown.

1946 The Winter Fair begins.

1950 Bozeman population tops 11,300.

1955 Bridger Bowl ski resort opens.

1965 Montana Agricultural College becomes Montana State University.

1966 Interstate highway system reaches Bozeman.

1960s–70s Urban Renewal leads to the demolition of downtown historic buildings in cities and towns nationwide, including Bozeman.

1978 Bozeman's first historic district, the South Willson Historic District (later the Bon Ton Historic District), is listed in the National Register of Historic Places.

1992 Bozeman's Conservation Overlay District, created with the intent of preserving buildings and streetscapes within broader Bozeman, is established.

SELECTED BIBLIOGRAPHY

Alderson, Matt. *Bozeman: A Guide to Its Places of Recreation and a Synopsis of Its Superior Natural Advantages, Industries, and Opportunities.* Bozeman: Avant-Courier Publishing Co., 1883.

Burlingame, Merrill G. *Gallatin Century of Progress.* Bozeman: Gallatin County Historical Society Publication, 1964.

———. "John M. Bozeman, Montana Trailmaker." *Mississippi Valley Historical Review* 27 (March 1941).

City of Bozeman, Montana. *Bozeman Unified Development Ordinance,* 2004.

———. *Guide to Sunset Hills Cemetery,* 2000.

———. *Historic Preservation* brochure, 2004.

———. *Neighborhood Conservation Overlay District* brochure, 2004.

———. Department of Planning. *Bozeman 2020 Community Plan,* 2001.

Doyle, Susan B., ed. *Journeys to the Land of Gold: Emigrant Diaries from the Bozeman Trail, 1863–1866.* 2 vols. Helena: Montana Historical Society Press, 2000.

Dunbar, Robert G. "The Economic Development of the Gallatin Valley." *Pacific Northwest Quarterly* (October 1956).

Ellsworth, W. E., ed. *A History of the Gallatin Valley and the City of Bozeman, with Sketches of Men, Firms and Corporations.* Bozeman: Avant-Courier Publishing Co., 1898.

Fenlason, Ed, and Mel Gemmill. *The Hills by the Headwaters.* Belgrade, Mt.: E and M Books, 1997.

Historic Bozeman and Gallatin County Montana: A Self-Guided Historical Tour. Bozeman: Historic Preservation Board of Gallatin County, 1999.

Historic Fire Insurance Maps of Bozeman, Montana, 1884, 1889, 1904, 1912, 1927, 1943. Sanborn Fire Insurance Company. http://sanborn.umi.com/.

Hoy, William S. *Railroad Stations in the Gallatin Area, Montana.* Germantown, Md.: Keystone Press, 1998.

"The Gallatin Valley, Montana." *The Coast,* 1908.

Indian Affairs in Gallatin County. Bozeman: Gallatin County Historical Society, n.d.

J. D. Radford and Company, *Gallatin Valley Gazetteer and Bozeman City Directory.* Bozeman: J. D. Radford & Co. New Issue Publishing, 1893.

Lee, Thomas, and B. Derek Strahn. *Historic Homes of Bozeman*. Bozeman: Bozeman Daily Chronicle, 2004.

McDonald, James R. *Bozeman Historic Resource Survey*. Missoula, Mt.: James R. McDonald Architects, 1984.

Montana State University Facilities Office. *Building and Architect Roster for MSU–Bozeman*. Bozeman, n.d.

Napton, Lewis K. "Canyon and Valley: Preliminary Archaeological Survey in the Gallatin Area, Montana." Thesis, University of Montana, Missoula, 1966.

O'Neill, Maire E. *Inventory of Historic Agricultural Structures in Gallatin County, Montana: A Pilot Survey*. Bozeman: Montana State University Department of Architecture, 1999.

R. L. Polk and Co. *Bozeman City Directory and Gallatin County Directory*. Helena and Butte: R. L. Polk & Co. of Montana, various years.

Smith, Phyllis. *Bozeman and the Gallatin Valley: A History*. Helena, Mt.: Falcon Press, 1996.

Strahn, B. Derek. *Bozeman Daily Chronicle At Home Magazine* articles. November 2000–December 2002.

Taylor, Dede. "The City Hall-Opera House: Bozeman's Civic Cathedral." Thesis, Montana State University–Bozeman, 2000.

Tracy, Sarah J. *Bozeman—1869: The Diary and Reminiscences of Mrs. William H. (Sarah J. Bessey) Tracy*. Bozeman: Gallatin Historical Society, 1985.

United States Department of the Interior. National Register of Historic Places Inventory—Nomination Forms for Bon Ton Historic District, Bozeman Brewery Historic District, Cooper Park Historic District, Gallatin Gateway Inn Historic District, Lindley Place Historic District, Main Street Historic District, North Tracy Avenue Historic District, Northern Pacific and Story Mill Historic District, South Tracy and South Black Historic District, South Tracy Avenue Historic District, Washington D.C., National Park Service. Copies on file at the State Historic Preservation Office, Helena.

Utley, Robert M. "The Bozeman Trail before John Bozeman." *Montana The Magazine of Western History* 53 (Summer 2003).

Williams, Lyle. *Historically Speaking: Stories of the Men and Women Who Explored and Settled the Missouri Headwaters*. Three Forks, Mt.: self-published, 1976.

INDEX OF SITES

Buildings without proper names are listed by historic district.